Multispecies Ethnography

Multispecies Ethnography

Methodology of a Holistic Research Approach of Humans, Animals, Nature, and Culture

Katharina Ameli

LEXINGTON BOOKS
Lanham • Boulder • New York • London

Published by Lexington Books
An imprint of The Rowman & Littlefield Publishing Group, Inc.
4501 Forbes Boulevard, Suite 200, Lanham, Maryland 20706
www.rowman.com

86-90 Paul Street, London EC2A 4NE

Copyright © 2022 by Katharina Ameli
Translated by Katharina Ameli with Julianna Leibold

British Library Cataloguing in Publication Information Available

Library of Congress Cataloging-in-Publication Data

Names: Ameli, Katharina, 1986- author.
Title: Multispecies ethnography : methodology of a holistic research approach
    of humans, animals, nature, and culture / [translated by] Katharina Ameli,
    [with Julianna Leibold].
Other titles: Multispezies-Ethnographie English
Description: Lanham, Maryland : Lexington Books, [2022] | Original work in
    German. | Includes bibliographical references and index.
Identifiers: LCCN 2022001884 (print) | LCCN 2022001885 (ebook) |
    ISBN 9781666911923 (Cloth : acid-free paper) | ISBN 9781666911947 (paperback) |
    ISBN 9781666911930 (ePub)
Subjects: LCSH: Ethnology—Bibliography. | Human-animal
    relationships—Bibliography.
Classification: LCC GN316 .M8613 2022 (print) | LCC GN316 (ebook) |
    DDC 305.8—dc23/eng/20220215
LC record available at https://lccn.loc.gov/2022001884
LC ebook record available at https://lccn.loc.gov/2022001885

∞™ The paper used in this publication meets the minimum requirements of American
National Standard for Information Sciences—Permanence of Paper for Printed Library
Materials, ANSI/NISO Z39.48-1992.

For Enzo

Contents

Acknowledgments

This book was largely written during a research stay in Canada and profited greatly from the results of previous research and interdisciplinary alliances in existing HumansAnimalsNaturesCultures.

The greatest thanks go to my long-time colleague and friend Anja Dulleck. She accompanied me in the creation of this book since day one and was always available for professional discussions and corrections to the manuscript.

In Canada, I am grateful to all the admirable colleagues, students, animals, and natural places that never stopped challenging me to develop the idea of multispecies research. Without the personal experiences and helpful conversations on campus and 'the land,' this book would not exist. I want to thank Terry Gibbs, Catherine O'Brien, Patrick Howard, and the Cape Breton Highland National Park with all its species as representatives.

I am also indebted to my colleagues in Gießen, each of whom looked at this work from their own discipline, for important hints and suggestions. I am thankful to Lisa Weber, Lea Benner, Stephanie Krämer, Thomas Brüsemeister, Anna Julia Schmidt, and Theresa Braun.

To my dear sister, Verena Wagner, and my colleague, Jaqueline Winkel, I thank you from the bottom of my heart for doing the final formal review of the manuscript.

A big thank you goes to my colleague, Julianna Leibold. She supported me actively in the translation and creation of the English version of this work, invested a lot of time, and her full dedication and ultimately took care of the final editing.

Special thanks go to Tracey Harris and Stephen Augustine. Tracey guided my entire research process over many years. She enabled me and my family to have a memorable journey with great experiences. And she was always available for professional exchanges and gave me time for this work.

I cannot thank Stephen enough for his invitation and the time he took to share his knowledge and recommend relevant literature for my project. Here I am also indebted to Diane Chisholm of the Mi'kmaq Resource Centre at Cape Breton University. She assisted me on many days with relevant, pre-selected literature for this work and knew quite intuitively what I needed. Wela'lin.

The very greatest thanks go with deep love to my family, who have enjoyed the time of researching together with me and shared the hardships of me writing over a long period of time.

I dedicate this book to Enzo. He has been part of my life for more than 13 years and has shaped my research direction significantly.

The book was translated from German into English under the contribution of Julianna Leibold.

Preface

My interest in ethnographic research has been very relevant for me for years. I unconsciously conducted my first nonscientific (auto-)ethnographic surveys as a teenager over the course of several years, in which I was working in a veterinary clinic. Here, I collected 'data' on human-animal relations as 'head notes,' which shaped my experiences with and views on human-animal relations significantly and set a foundation for my book.

I conducted my first scientifically ethnographic research as part of my master's thesis. I wanted to highlight a section of human-animal relations and analyze more precisely the practice of dogs in the social settings of elderly care in nursing homes. The classical ethnography, which I used for this purpose, did not allow me to obtain the view I was striving for. Admittedly, the animal's point of view did not remain completely hidden from me and I was able to approach it significantly. However, the attribution of animals as belonging to nature as well as the classification that the related analyses were described as belonging to the natural sciences did not allow me sufficient points of contact at that time. The lack of necessary differentiated knowledge about the agency of dogs as well as the unanswered question of how to methodically include dogs in sociological research prevented a first implementation of a multispecies ethnography.

With many questions in mind and initial ideas for this work, I began to network further in an interdisciplinary way. I found partners in the discipline of veterinary medicine, as the importance of animal welfare plays a crucial role in it.

The insights into the disciplinary culture of veterinary medicine, but also their perspective on humans, animals, animal welfare and animal law, enabled me to broaden my perspective. This new perspective helped me realize that sociological research and natural sciences are highly interconnected.

The combining of already explored ethological knowledge of species research with the practice of ethnographic research allowed me to get my first impressions of what a multispecies ethnography could look like. The combination of both research approaches enabled me to give voice to animals and natures as well as to analyze social phenomena in a transformative way. The inclusion of animals and natures in the research methodology allowed me to involve them concretely with their agency, behavior, and individual needs and to expand my own methodological research action through a change of perspective.

However, in the further course and with the increasing impulses from other disciplines (including law, philosophy, business administration, cultural studies, and history) in the context of projects and courses, the agency of animals as well as the change of perspective did not seem clear enough to me. By this, I do not mean that there was no literature on the subject. Rather, I felt there was a lack of important thoughts, transformations, and results from interdisciplinary dialogues that would have discussed a multispecies methodology that included animal agency. Moreover, at present, the existing dichotomy between humans and animals and nature and culture in sociology is hardly related to the methodological orientation in the exclusion of animals. This exclusion is largely found in biomedical research as well, since the consideration of individuality and agency of animals is hardly reflected in the research of this field. Therefore, an application of multispecies ethnography in other fields, such as veterinary medicine or education, is of great interest to me in order to engage disciplines to build a more compassionate culture concerning their research involving animals and natures.

I chose the concept of HumansAnimalsNaturesCultures as an inclusive theoretical idea, which highlights and values the 'significant otherness' of the individual components.

The debates of exclusion, oppression, and commercialization of animals in the methodology of research in different disciplines have so far—under the aspect in the change of methodology—remained largely marginal.

Admittedly, critical animal studies already points out essential core elements of political action and addresses a moral commitment to animals. The building blocks of the concrete empirical approach in the implementation of a multispecies ethnography, which enables students to acquire related skills, have remained largely absent. It was therefore logical to consider multispecies ethnography in a differentiated way and to present it as an interdisciplinary methodology. By making this methodology accessible in the form of this book, scholars from all disciplines receive new impulses and, hopefully, are encouraged to engage in a more compassionate relationship with animals and natures.

My intensive research was supported through a research stay in Canada, where I originally wanted to analyze the roles of animals in Nature and Outdoor Learning with the help of multispecies ethnography.

The interdependencies in the context of human, animal, and nature relationships already illustrate a high level of complexity in the interdependencies between humans, animals, and natures. It quickly became clear to me that not only animals and their agency are excluded from the research, but also natures. For this reason, human-animal studies and NaturesCultures should function as a theoretical basis to establish the inclusion of the agency of natures and animals in an overall research concept.

I understand multispecies ethnography as a mosaic whose design is still in process and can and must always be further developed through (inter-) disciplinary research. Any ethical reflection of researchers concerning the relationships between humans, animals, and natures allows to make inequalities in the categorization of (disciplinary) structures and cultures visible and to reflect on the problems this raises in terms of social justice for multispecies actors. In this context, the close link between the categorization and structures of domination and power is extremely relevant.

It was therefore of great concern to me to map the methodology and method of multispecies ethnography in such a way that the perspective and needs of natures and animals are placed at the center of the research, so that points of contact for animal liberation and animal protection arise. This is not only relevant for cultural or social science disciplines but also for disciplines that claim to always generate objective and reliable data.

I see an essential piece of the mosaic of multispecies ethnography in indigenous theory as indigenous theories of natures, animals, and the interdependencies between humans and the more-than-human world represent a significant and currently largely unconsidered area when it comes to the agency of animals and natures in research methods. Thus, the inclusion of indigenous theories, as defined by Kincheloe and Steinberg (2008), is described as a scientifically compatible worldview that allows for complexity and multi-locality of multispecies ethnography.

The inclusion of indigenous theories in the form of referencing publications and research projects allows for new perspectives to be taken, enabling both a micro-perspective view of individual actors and a macro-perspective view of complex natures and cultures.

The multiple crises of the 21st century cannot be solved by debates within individual disciplines. The interdependencies between the fields are so close that they can only be countered by interdisciplinary dialogues and solution strategies.

Finally, the courage to reflect on the idea of (one's own) objectivity allows to question one's own subjective perception and to open up to animal and nature perspectives. I hope that this openness can have a positive impact on the fields of animal liberation and animal welfare as well as, in the sense of Kopnina, contribute to promoting a planetary citizenship that sufficiently takes into account the rights, individuality, and agency of animals and natures in research and everyday social life. The first step is to create a radically more compassionate culture in research with animals and natures by highlighting and valuing 'significant otherness' of individual actors. This means that characteristics that distinguish actors of the human and more-than-human worlds do not lead to distinction.

Overall, the work pursues the overarching goal of social justice as it addresses the interconnectedness of the well-being of natures, animals, and humans. multispecies ethnography helps centralize this view and the needs of natures and animals in research, which connects it to animal liberation and advocacy. It furthermore links various disciplines and hopefully encourages interdisciplinarity. I believe that multispecies ethnography can be applied in a way that highlights intersectionality and enables researchers across disciplines to center it in their work. For this intersectionality and interdisciplinarity, the discussion of indigenous theory and science is incredibly relevant to multispecies ethnography.

The book aims to open a critical interdisciplinary dialogue to established routines and to shape an inclusive and socially just world, which allows a well-being of natures, animals, and humans in different cultures in our (scientific) society.

Chapter 1

Introduction

The multiple crises of the beginning 21st century, which include climate change, habitat destruction, environmental pollution, species extinction, inequalities, and scarcity of resources (Statista 2018), as well as the corona pandemic, cause intense but also relevant debates in various disciplines, such as sociology, political sciences, natural sciences, or veterinary medicine (Jarass 2009; Segerer 2018; Stehr 2019).

It is remarkable that the relationships[1] between humans, animals,[2] and animate, as well as inanimate nature,[3] as a whole are rarely being connected. There are currently analyses of individual sub-segments, such as the perception of nature (e.g., Braun 2000; Becker 2016), the attribution of roles to animals (e.g., Sebastian 2017; Arluke and Sanders 1996; Johnson and Degeling 2012) or the aspect of the exploitation, and perception of nature and animals (Bläske 2019; Plumwood 2002, 8–10). However, an interdisciplinary and holistic approach to the analysis of the relations between humans, animals, and animate and inanimate nature still represents a blind spot.

Although a holistic approach is not yet available, the currently existing analyses and debates have already laid the foundation for the relations between humans and nature or humans and animals to increasingly come into focus in scientific, public, and political discourse (e.g., Fenske 2016, 298; Pschera 2014, 49; Ogdden et al. 2013; Hamilton and Taylor 2017; Jones 2019; Gesing et al. 2019).[4] Pschera states, for example, that the sensory perception and explanation of the environment, which plays a role especially in educational processes, is missing. Without a deeper understanding, prompted through education, it is almost impossible to discover animate and inanimate nature. According to Pschera, through theoretical and rationalized processing, children hardly ever consciously go into the forest and no longer touch or pick up animals for fear of touching them (in the wrong way). An averting and demarcation is said to have moved in place of inexperienced discoveries, which in the long run leads to a "compensation of nature consciousness" (Pschera 2014, 40). This prevents sensual contact with nature and animals, and the possibility of adequately describing nature and animal encounters is inhibited by the lack of appropriate language. This causes an alienation of nature through idealized views that focus on beauty and aesthetics and thus disregard essential 'unattractive' features of nature. Pschera illustrates this with the example of a female brown bear with offspring in the Hellabrunn Zoo: Visitors with children observe the little bears at the bear enclosure and clarify their fascination with 'Ahhs' and 'Ohs.' Unexpectedly, a group of ducks flies up and lands in the moat of the bear enclosure. The female bear "does not hesitate for a second. She plunges into the water, sweeps the group of ducks apart with a stroke of her paw and devours the small birds" (Pschera 2014, 40). The shocked spectators are described as crying children and shocked parents who try to explain what happened. Pschera states that the situation leaves the other visitors, but also Pschera himself, to question whether this really is nature (Pschera, 40). He concludes that this open question is closely linked to mechanisms of demarcation, alienation, and exclusion (Pschera, 40).

Both the analysis of these mechanisms and the interdependencies of humans, animals, nature, and cultures will have to be examined in greater depth in the future through concrete research, so that in addition to the questions of content, existing and implemented research methods and approaches will have to be reflected upon and rethought in a transformative way against the background of interdisciplinary research work and methods. This goal is already being pursued, for example, in human-animal studies or in the analyses of NaturesCultures.

Daumiller (2017) attributes the strong interest of scientists in these fields to an intentional motivation. The love of animals, the mission of animal protection, nature conservation, or animal rights, all are biographically shaped and promote the orientation toward this research topic. Plumwood criticizes, however, the form of monological and dualistic thinking in the scientific debates conducted so far, which radically distinguish scientists (Plumwood 2002, 45).

In the scientific context, however, the analysis of relationships and relations between humans, nature, and animals cannot be carried out by a single discipline. Rather, the complexity of the subject matter makes it possible to identify essential connections in the differences and similarities of these relationships. Sociology, political science, philosophy, education, natural science, or veterinary medicine can jointly and separately research and analyze the connection between humans, animals, and the animate and inanimate environment in different dimensions.

However, a glance at the various disciplines shows that nature and animals are construed differently in each case (for more detailed information see chapter 2). In addition, nature and animals and their interaction with society are described in the form of dualisms[5] (Plumwood 2002). Although these dualisms and the exclusion of nature and animals or humans are described as outdated in various research projects, the number of interdisciplinary research projects on the topic is still small (Kompatscher et al. 2017). Due to the structure of research funding allocation, there are hardly any opportunities for funding, especially for cross-border projects involving nature and animals in an innovative manner (Bendix and Bizer 2011, 3–5). This can possibly be attributed to the fact that their transformative character cannot be defined clearly enough and many unknowns remain (Fenske 2016, 216).

Last but not least, the anchoring of the methodological approach also plays a decisive role in the planning and implementation of research projects. In order to exemplify, we will look at the veterinary medical discipline. For instance, this discipline hardly ever uses qualitative procedures in the analysis of experiments with animals but focuses exclusively on standardized procedures 'with reliable findings.' The intention of veterinarians to use qualitative methods (e.g., in research on laboratory animals) would at first glance probably raise structural questions on research in the scientific community and make it unlikely to receive funding due to the lack of reliable results.[6]

The current debates mark a shift toward topics concerning nature, animals, and their interaction with humans. However, a deeper examination shows that relations between humans and animals or humans and nature are primarily being treated in specific fields such as 'human-animal studies' or 'NaturesCultures'.

HUMAN-ANIMAL RELATION

Although the variety of relationships between humans and animals has always been changing and is characterized by ambivalent conditions, the number of personal relationships with (domestic) animals as well as the industrial production of animals for food purposes has steadily increased (Sebastian and Gutjahr 2014, 116). Especially the instrumentalization and use of animals in the food industry is analyzed sociologically (Sebastian 2017; Harris 2017).

Animals are assigned different roles: Thus, they are understood as 'commodities' that are strategically marketed and bred to provide the best possible benefit for humans. This is justified, not just with the economic orientation, but also with the maintenance of human health. Parallel to this, there is an advanced love of animals, which allows selected animals to live as partners, family members or assistants in therapeutic or pedagogical work

(Ameli 2016, 1). These partnerships are often lived out through identities. Deeply felt sympathies and needs are linked to the animal and influence one's own identity (Jones 2019, 300).

Animals almost naturally take on different roles in very different areas of people's everyday lives. It is therefore not surprising that researchers from various disciplines are currently interested in the analysis of existential and collective relationships between humans and animals. Over the past 25 years, relevant insights have been gained in this area. For example, routines of human encounters with animals in private households, animal shelters, zoos, or large farms have been analyzed as well as laboratory and close-to-nature encounters (Alger and Alger 2003; Ameli 2016; Arluke and Sanders 1996; Bläske 2019; Patronek 2008; Philipps 2008).

In retrospect, the human-animal relationship can be traced back to role attributions and views of animals that have emerged through cultural and religious as well as social developments in society. At the same time, the observation and domestication of animals has shaped the image of these very animals (Cyrulnik et al. 2003, 10; Otterstedt 2003, 15; Mütherich 2004, 21–25).

Gutjahr and Sebastian deplore the lack of a more advanced and in-depth analysis of social human-animal relations, especially for the sociological discipline. According to the authors, the extent to which animals are used and instrumentalized has changed considerably in recent decades. Social processes are not sufficiently analyzed under due consideration of cultural and social functions of animals in Germany (Gutjahr and Sebastian 2014, 57–60). In the sociological discipline, only Birgit Mütherich (2004), Marcel Mauss (2013), and Rainer Wiedenmann (2009) show a deeper involvement of animals in social contexts by perceiving them as actors.[7] Wiedenmann (2009) formulates social human-animal relationships on the macro level as "human-animal sociality." This implies that animals are conceived as actors (2009, 68) and that human-animal relationships are not "natural, but (. . .) change-able" (2009, 28). "It should be possible to record human-animal interactions in such a way that the behavioral processes of primary micro-sociology can at least to some extent be linked or mediated with the intermediate meso-level (. . .) and the social macro-level" (2009, 107). This complexity in the analysis must be countered with theories and interpretations that prevent cer-tain 'social techniques' in the individual disciplines from tempting people to avoid dealing with complex and ambivalent issues (2009, 75).

In addition, conflicting relationships and role assignments between humans and animals are usually strongly linked to human needs. This results from the position of power that humans hold by deciding when and how they treat an animal (Buchner-Fuhs 1999, 275 ff). This treatment not only relates to the classic fields of agriculture but also plays a role in private households, which should not be underestimated. Domestic animal husbandry is therefore also increasingly coming into the focus of research projects. For example, psychological studies have found that the abuse of animals is associated with an increased risk of child abuse (Degue and Dilillo 2009). In addition, both the consumption of so-called farm animals (Sebastian and Gutjahr 2014) and the use of laboratory animals for scientific purposes have long been discussed (Krämer 2019). Last but not least, the relevance of animals in therapeutic and educational work areas has been increasingly discussed in recent years (Ameli et al. 2016). The rescue of animals from shelters, too, has been examined from various perspectives (e.g., Alger and Alger 2003; Arluke et al. 1999).

HUMAN-NATURE RELATION

In addition to the analysis of relationships between humans and animals, the area of the human-nature relationship—in which animals may be integrated depending on the discipline—is also discussed. It should be noted here that the analysis of the human-nature relationship seems to be older than analyses of the human-animal relationship. This can be attributed to the fact that animals were initially described as part of nature (Bell 2012; Reichhold 2016).

In everyday life, nature is often described both as the original or good and as the wild and threatening (Groß 2006, 5). In scientific discourses, the concept of nature is not uniformly defined, either. For example, Gebhard describes nature as a totality of "natural phenomena, i.e. animals, plants, landscape" (2013, 40), while Mackert and Petrisch see nature as a "dynamic interaction of natural and human forces of movement and shaping" (2016, 21). Last but not least, nature has an aesthetic dimension, in which the symbolic meaning of nature is particularly at home (Gebhard 2013, 49). This results from a strategy—in addition to religion and economically pragmatic approaches—which aims at understanding nature in its depths (Cobern 2000).

The debates in the context of the Anthropocene[8] state that nature is shaped to a large extent by humans, so that society, culture, and nature can no longer be regarded separately (Springer 2016). This is influenced by advances in digitization and technology, in which nature is understood as an 'embedded system' consisting of human as hardware and nature as software. Both subareas are only functional if they are coordinated with each other (Pschera 2014, 155; Mackert and Petrisch 2016, 21).

The increase in digitization and technological progress also causes a reformation of the understanding of nature. Pschera assumes that the future understanding of nature as well as the exploration of nature will be bound to various technological processes more than ever (Pschera 2014, 155).[9]

Chapter 1

This development is accompanied by the need for ambivalence tolerance. This includes that a resilience of nature should be created and subsequently maintained. The concept of a resilience of nature characterizes in detail natural areas that are developed in a targeted manner using technical methods. Through this, nature is apparently saved from technology and civilization. Conversely, however, this means that a (different) construction of nature results (Pschera 2014, 165). This can be explained using the example of corals. With the help of a variety of technical aids, heat-resistant corals are bred in order to counteract the progressive warming of the world's oceans and the destruction of coral reefs by increasingly frequent 'bleaching events.' However, their invasive spread may cause other coral species to be displaced (Preston 2019). Although the theoretical coordination of nature appears to be functional this way, it remains unpredictable in many areas (Pschera 2014, 155, 163–164; Fenske 2016, 191).

HUMAN-ANIMAL-NATURE-BOND

Shifts and reorientation in the construction of nature and animals are tied to negotiation processes that play a decisive role in shaping the attribution of roles to animals and other actors in a more-than-human world (Fenske 2016, 298).[10] In this way, the view of animals, nature, and humans is shaped differently, resulting in a variety of overlapping, intersecting, and competing constructions of nature and animals. According to Pschera, these changes and adaptations are key to future changes in perspectives and enable us to break new ground (Pschera 2014, 300). At the same time, the very "idea of the idea of nature" (Pschera 2014, 135) leads to the loss of constructed realities and consequently to the fact that there will be "no way back to ['original] nature'" (Pschera 2014, 49–51). The discussion about changing constructions of nature and animals by humans is linked to the debate about the existence of dichotomies between humans / nature / animals. At the same time, their softening in different contexts is discussed by scientists (Hamilton and Taylor 2017, 6–7; Chimaira Arbeitskreis 2011; Mütherich 2004). Hamilton and Taylor point out that the critical examination of possible dichotomies between humans and animals or humans and nature is not very helpful. According to them, an animal in the narrower sense is not human[11] and a plant is not an animal (Hamilton and Taylor 2017, 6–8). Nebelung also shares this view and, in his work 'Ökologische Theorien' (Ecological Theories, 2003), describes the interdependence of humans and nature from a sociological and biological perspective as follows: "Humans [are] nature. When they talk about it, they do so linguistically. And we must assign the personal language—even if it is difficult—to culture, even if it has a biological core" (Nebelung 2003, 12).

According to Hamilton and Taylor, the elimination of dichotomies misses the goal of recognizing the specifics of the relationship and the importance and agency of each individual—whether human, animal, or plant. The two authors therefore call for the establishment of an inclusive understanding that recognizes the otherness and difference of nature and animals. This recognition is to be taken into account especially in research projects and their results and is achieved through a high degree of freedom and the joy of experimentation (Hamilton and Taylor 2017, 6–8). Categories are not to be described as something negative, but allow the uniqueness of being of nature and animals to be appreciated. What remains open here is how nature and animals are ultimately made tangible and how a consensus of categories is developed (Hamilton and Taylor 2017, 45).

Kaldewey adds that within the discussions about the abolition of dichotomies, dualisms would automatically arise that could only be answered if philosophical and epistemological questions were to be included (Kaldewey 2008, 282). Here, an existing, practiced dualism in society makes it possible to perceive it as a dimension of social reality and to place it in the research contexts (Kaldewey 2011, 284).

Pschera goes even further here by stating that in order to resolve dichotomies, one must above all answer unpleasant questions. One focus should be on the alienation of humans from nature—which he describes as triggered by animal protection, species protection, and nature conservation (Pschera 2014, 40). In contrast, there is a generation of young people formulating emphatic demands concerning their future and in doing so make special reference to environmental and climate protection (Albert et al. 2019).

The assumption that an increasing alienation of nature has been shaped by rigid boundaries in everyday life is the only consensus. This can be observed in the example of children and young people's experiences of nature. The changed way in which humans interact with nature, for example, is caused by the lack of haptic contact with nature and animals, which is relevant for educational processes (Pschera 2014, 40; Gebhard 2013). The recommendation to instead practice exclusive observation as opposed to direct and sensual contact with animate and inanimate nature ultimately leads to a "nature-animalist inclusion dilemma" for nature and animals (Pschera 2014, 126). Nature and animals are excluded by humans and society because as systems they do not come into direct contact. As an example of this finding, Pschera cites what is known as 'bird watching,' that is, simply looking at or observing birds in their natural habitat. Bird watchers, that is, the persons actively observing birds, have top-class equipment for close contact with birds (e.g., functional clothing and binoculars). However, this closeness is only imaginary, as it rather indicates an external distance (Pschera, 41–44). It should be noted here, however, that a lack of equipment would prevent contact with the birds per se, as they would otherwise be little or hardly visible. In the context of pure observation of wildlife, it is rather assumed that there is no focus on haptic contact, but that the distance is respected, which makes concrete observations possible in the first place (Pschera 2014, 41–43; Strunz 2013, 159–161). Nature is consequently not, as often thought, wild and free, but in some way always influenced or constructed by human (Subramaniam 2019, 192–194).

TRANSFORMATIVE MULTISPECIES RESEARCH

The developments described suggest that the imbalance and asymmetry in the consideration of nature and animals in scientific research must be reflected on more strongly. As a consequence, it is necessary that in future a fair representation and adequate consideration of nature and animals in transformative research and educational processes is pursued in order to adequately open up different versions of reality. This includes questioning common patterns of behavior, such as the status of animals as 'companion animals' or 'commodities,' and investigating how animals or nature tell stories. According to Hamilton and Taylor, an ethnographic methodology—Multispecies Ethnography—is particularly suitable for this purpose, especially for depicting narratives of animals and nature: Their appearance, history, personality, moods, charisma, and experienced events up to 'death' are taken into account (Hamilton and Taylor 2017, 177; Fudge 2017, 5).[12] This requires both a pronounced capacity for empathy and an inclusive attitude toward animals and nature (Hamilton and Taylor 2017, 177).

Multispecies Ethnography does not yet represent an established methodology, although a paradigm shift in research with nature and animals can be assumed. It is therefore necessary to further develop the methodology and to test it in practice and in interdisciplinary contexts. In addition to established findings from various disciplines, indigenous knowledge on sensory observations must be included. The present book aims to take up this desideratum and integrate indigenous theory into the methodology of observing multispecies.

The special feature of Multispecies Ethnography is that it analyzes the actions of individual actors (Atkinson et al. 2001; Delamont 2012; Pole and Morrison 2003; Breidenstein 2006) in interactions between humans, nature, and animals, thus promising new possibilities in the research of innovative questions. Currently, relationships between elephants and their trainers (Locke 2012), beekeepers and bees (Kosut and Moore 2016; Fenske 2017), children and insects (Taylor and Pacini-Ketchabaw 2015), humans and cats in animal shelters (Alger and Alger 2003), and interactions between children and animals in schools have already been analyzed (Pedersen 2010;

Levinson et al. 2017). Last but not least, David Abram's work (2010), 'Becoming Animal,' can be seen as an important resource in the further development of Multispecies Ethnography. This results from his authentic descriptions in contact with nature and animals, which he documents and understands as essential basic elements of future multispecies research.

Multispecies Ethnography not only is a methodology for analyzing the relationships between humans, animals, and nature but also provides theoretical contributions that reconceptualize what it ultimately means to be human (Ogden et al. 2013, 7). The analysis of this question will be tried out in a differentiated way as a transformative procedure representing Multispecies Ethnography and further developed in an interdisciplinary dialogue in order to modify current methodological approaches and adequately include animals and nature (Gesing et al. 2019, 27).

AIM AND STRUCTURE OF THIS BOOK

The basis of this work is the hypothesis of inclusive HumansAnimalsNatures-Cultures (see chapter 3).[13] The assumption that a collaborative, inter- and multi-disciplinary cooperation and consideration of the complexity of nature, humans, and animals exists results from the interface consideration between social- and natural science-oriented disciplines. Thus, this book is preceded by a vision that seeks to question holistically how scientists can integrate nature and animals into research projects through Multispecies Ethnography.

It is therefore essential that the following work takes into account sociological, educational, natural scientific, and veterinary theories and perspectives in order to point out similarities. Since different disciplines intersect within multispecies research, the piloting of the theoretical derivation will be concentrated into a methodology that allows an analysis of HumansAnimalsNaturesCultures in both interdisciplinary and disciplinary contexts. For this reason, the methodology of Multispecies Ethnography—which is already being carried out by some scientists—will be analyzed with regard to the disciplines described and finally be comprehensively developed methodically as a holistic approach. Here, it can be assumed that in addition to humans, animals, plants, and animate and inanimate nature, digital contexts such as robots or the so-called Internet of Animals[14] (Pschera 2014) will be taken into account as multispecies actors. This results from the fact that all the actors described are able to carry out (social) interactions in different ways. Exemplary findings in this respect are provided by the research fields of human-animal studies, NaturesCultures, environmental sociology, or related fields of research. The example of NaturesCultures can illustrate this inclusion once again: Jones' concept describes an inclusive view in which animals in landscapes embody nature and demonstrate the close connection between the two (Jones 2019, 298). This insight allows a combination of theories and descriptions with deeply felt sympathies, commitments, and affiliations for the more-than-human world (Hacking 2000, 68–70; Jones 2019, 298), so that the close connection between the areas of humans, animals, nature, and cultures can be identified.

The present work is based on precisely this concept: The introductory chapter has already shown in some areas the importance of (future) human-animal-nature interactions and the blind spot that currently exists in research methodology. Thus, first of all, the theoretical approach to nature and animals from the four different disciplines of sociology, educational science, natural science, and veterinary medicine is analyzed (chapter 2). Based on this (inter-)disciplinary contextual consideration, the concept of HumansAnimalsNaturesCultures is introduced is based on and extends the results of the dialogues in human-animal studies and NaturesCultures (chapter 3). Following on from this, the methodology of Multispecies Ethnography is elaborated in accordance with classical ethnography. Relevant characteristics of the methodology will be identified in order to make them usable for Multispecies Ethnography, so that all actors and actants, that is, humans, animals, and plants (and robots), can be included.

With the help of empirical results from conducted multispecies ethnographies, the methodology will be supported by the examples and the theoretical construction will be condensed. From this, a model is to be developed that can be used in the future as a basis for analyses, both in the empirical research of HumansAnimalsNaturesCultures and in the relevant subareas of the holistic analysis of relationships between humans, animals, and nature (chapter 4). The focus will be on the behavior, challenges, and opportunities of researchers in the field as well as on their needs and expectations. For this purpose, a research design of a Multispecies Ethnography research in the context of nature- and animal-based education is documented as an example (chapter 6). This results in a systematic derivation of the methodology, which highlights opportunities and limitations.

In accordance with Dwelling and Prus (2012), the present work is a guide to a new and innovative form of ethnographic multispecies research. The work does not claim to describe the pure theory of Multispecies Ethnography. Rather, it is a posthuman Multispecies Ethnography that is intended to serve as a stimulus for future research in the field of human-animal studies, nature-related educational processes and interdisciplinary research projects. The documented conceptions and suggestions are not to be understood as final, but rather represent the beginning of a process-like development toward an increased consideration of animals and the animate and inanimate environment—the so-called more-than-human world[15]—in ethnographic multispecies research. They can be used for future research projects and give rise to expectations of innovative results for HumansAnimalsNaturesCultures in (inter-) disciplinary contexts.

NOTES

1. In this work, the terms 'relationships' and 'relations' are used synonymously, since both describe an interaction between humans, animals, and animate and inanimate nature. I understand these relationships as reciprocal relations, which are characterized by political, cultural, private, intra-, and inter-specific relationships.

2. In the debate on speciesism and in publications of human-animal studies, the term 'nonhuman animals' is often used to emphasize that humans are also animals (Dunayer 2001). The following work has chosen to use the term 'animal(s)' without affirming a dichotomy in the sense of Hamilton and Taylor (2017). Rather, it emphasizes the uniqueness and individuality of nonhuman animals. This stands for itself in the use of the term 'animal(s)' and allows the disciplines to connect to Multispecies Ethnography. Categories are not to be described as something negative per se, but allow to appreciate the uniqueness of being nature and animal.

3. For the sake of completeness, it must also be noted that some sources assume that animals are included in the concept of nature (e.g., Gebhard 2013, 40).

4. This leads to the thesis that the importance of these debates has been further underlined by the corona crisis. For example, the lockdown showed a change in earth movements (Gibney 2020) and suggests that further effects and consequences will emerge in the coming years. Here, Multispecies Ethnography could play a relevant role, as it recognizes the transfer between disciplines and the recognition of the virus in its interaction with nature, humans, and animals.

5. Dualisms are particularly evident in the dichotomy of social actions. In the example of animals, this becomes clear through their role as pets on the one hand and their role as livestock on the other.

6. Nevertheless, the SET Foundation—as probably the first funding institution in Germany—has shown great openness toward funding such a qualitative pilot project in 2020. It approved qualitative research at a 3Rs center in order to promote the objective of establishing alternative and complementary methods through a culture of care.

7. The term 'actors' is treated in this work not as a personal designation, but as an abstraction.

8. The Anthropocene is discussed as a new geological age, which assumes that modern humans and their technological innovations have a significant impact on the climate and the environment. Existing and central concepts, relationships, and separations—especially between nature and culture—are questioned (Springer 2016; Crutzen 2000; Crutzen and Stoermer 2002). (Sociological) analyses of the concept of the Anthropocene are examined in greater depth by Laux and Henkel (2018).

9. One form of this understanding of nature can be called 'digital nature,' after Yoichi Ochiai. This describes a new perspective on nature that is composed of digital media. The future in form of digital media describes alternatives both to our nature

and to the way we perceive it (Digital Nature Group n.d.). An example of the concrete implementation refers to the digital nature studies, which analyze the importance of digital contacts with nature (van Houwelingen-Snippe et al. 2020).

10. These negotiation processes and the changing constructions of nature and animals will consequently also become relevant for educational processes in terms of nature and animals, as the lack of contact of children with nature has been discussed for several years (Mitscherlich 1965, 25; Gebhard 2013, 36; Hüther 2005, 2008). This implies at the same time the necessity of a reflection on nature-based learning and animal-supported education.

11. This is where the scientific debate reveals relevant opposing views. These result on the basis of biological sameness or else differences (Glock 2016, 13–15; Manser 2016, 23–25).

12. In the past, language has often been named—especially in sociology—as the decisive argument for classifying animals and nature as being external (Mütherich 2004). The call for ethnographic multispecies research invalidates this argument, since Multispecies Ethnography uses language as an element to include the more-than-human world. Thus, it allows to reconstruct the context of relations between humans, nature, and animals (Abram 2010).

13. In the sense of Gesing et al. (2019), a combination of two terms such as natures and cultures can be irritating. A fusion of four terms can further intensify this irritation, since, although these terms occur together both scientifically and in every-day use, they are not used as one combined word. Nevertheless, it is precisely this fusion that is intended to depict the interrelationships and the dimensions linked to them. By this, the inseparability of the research areas should be made clear. Further, especially in (inter-)disciplinary contexts, individual strands of research within HumansAnimalsNaturesCultures are still taken into account, which still guarantees the individuality of the fields. According to Gesing (2019, 8–9), the plural for human beings, animals, natures, and cultures results from Latours (1995, 139–140) recognition that nature and culture are not arbitrary and identical, but rather different. This means that there is a shift away from a universal nature and toward natures (Gesing et al. 2019, 7).

14. The "Internet of Animals" describes the tracking and tracing of animals via transmitters or cameras by feeding the acquired data into the internet. The internet itself can be characterized as foreign to nature because it represents a machine. Pschera (2014, 44–47) describes an internet of people, an internet of things, and an internet of animals. The assumption of an internet of animals implies that animals on the internet must also be understood as individuals who have a right to protection and optimal living conditions. This raises the question of whether data protection regulations for animals would also be necessary. At the same time, the question remains open as to whether humans, for example, receive a realistic image of a real setting when they are in virtual proximity to a polar bear or a tiger, and whether this proximity can really replace meaningful experiences in extra-digital settings.

15. The term 'more-than-human world' was especially coined by David Abram. He describes the relation to the earthly world (Abram 1996).

Chapter 2

Humans, Animals, and Nature in (Inter-)disciplinary Contexts

A close connection between humans, animals, nature, and culture is hardly doubted at present, even though dichotomies between humans and animals or nature and culture have been reproduced by research areas and disciplinary theories (e.g., Kompatscher et al. 2017; Wiedenmann 2009; Bell 2012). The establishment of research areas that focus on the interconnectedness of the fields shows a thematization and analysis of nature and animals often within two separate areas. For example, NaturesCultures, environmental sociology, or human-animal studies integrate nature or animals as actors of the more-than-human world into their analyses within their research contexts.

According to Gesing et al. (2019, 18–20), following these developments, a species turn has already become established, which allows old patterns to be reformulated and transformative concepts to be applied. In order to demonstrate both the significance of this species turn and the importance of the disciplines for this turn, the following section documents the consideration of exemplarily selected disciplines. This is understood as an essential basis for specifying future (multispecies) research.

Using sociology, pedagogy, natural sciences, and veterinary medicine as examples, similarities and differences in the understanding of nature and animals are worked out and relevant areas of contact are presented. These are seen as the foundation for a transformation in interdisciplinary research on HumansAnimalsNaturesCultures, without resetting the value of each individual discipline.

The following chapter does not pursue an encyclopedic treatment of all relevant topics of the chosen disciplines but focuses on essential subareas that exemplify the core areas of the respective discipline and illustrate their importance for (interdisciplinary) future multispecies research.

2.1 HUMANS, ANIMALS, AND
NATURE IN SOCIOLOGY

The sociological consideration in the context of multispecies research goes back to the question whether current crises and problems can be adequately explained as long as a separation of nature and culture or humans and animals prevails in the sociological discipline (Gesing et al. 2019, 7). This means that the suitability of the various approaches for nature and animals must be questioned.

Nature is described by Nebelung as a social construct that can be both threatening and beautiful at the same time. This so-called "social beyond is (. . .) decorated, shaped, ordered and thus becomes part of society" (Nebelung 2003, 160). Marx, on the other hand, in his concept of nature, assumes a natural relationship that conditions the generation of living conditions. This results from the assumption that natural foundations are changed and that close connections to the concept of work result. This implies an appropriation of nature by humans and leads to a utilization process (Dörhöfer 2003, 36–37).

The understanding of nature as a social construct is described by Brand and Reusswig (2020) as a constructivist or culturalistic perspective. Humans, animals, and nature are not independent variables in relation to each other, but are determined by social discourse. This contrasts with the realistic or naturalistic view of human-nature-animal relations, which is increasingly found in the natural science disciplines. These differences in the disciplines ultimately led to the classification of humans as belonging to the social realm and thus to the distinction between human beings and animals, as well as the corresponding laws (Block 2016, 12).

In earlier writings of the 20th century, approaches to biosociological analogy formation and the attempt to establish a sociology of animals have already been practiced. Here, a transfer of human-sociological categories was to be established (Alverdes 1925), which, however, led to an analogization of nature, animals, and humans. Biological and social actions as analogy were still critically examined due to the self-conception of sociology, so that this research area remained marginalized (Wiedenmann 2009, 62). This initially led to the exclusion of nature and animals from sociological analyses and to a further reception of the dichotomy in the human-animal sociality or so-called relationship between humans, nature, and animals (Wiedenmann 2009; Mütherich 2004; Chimaira Arbeitskreis 2011; Bell 2012).

The separation of nature and animals is not surprising for Wiedenmann, since he considers the sociological concept of nature to be unsuitable for a human-animalistic sociality (Wiedenmann 2009, 67). With the question "What do animals actually have to do with sociology?" (Wiedenmann 2009, 17) he illustrates the oblivion toward animals in his own discipline and at the same time points out the constant dichotomy between humans, nature, and animals. In the field of human-animal relations, this is primarily due to the fact that pressing questions cannot be fitted into the corset of rigid dichotomies and that this has led to a 'sociological helplessness' for many years, which was first questioned by Bryant (1979) and Arluke (1993) in their own discipline, by questioning the dichotomy between humans and animals (Wiedenmann 2009, 17). While human-animal sociality in particular then became a serious area of research in English-speaking sociology, German-speaking sociology still lags behind today (Wiedenmann 2009, 17; Gutjahr and Sebastian 2014, 57–59).

Animals are described as inferior beings by Mead (1980, 140), as nonhuman beings by Weber (1984, 3), as different individuals by Marx (Mütherich 2004, 74) and as suffering beings in critical theory (Sebastian and Gutjahr 2014, 116).

Mütherich attributes this view of animals to the strongly philosophical view of Weber, Marx, and the Frankfurt School, who assume that human-animal relationships describe a social construct in which animals are not capable of social action (Mütherich 2004, 67–69). This view results from a distrust of the methodological recording of animal behavior. In the further process—favored by the social situation—a tabooing of animals in the sociology was established (Mütherich, 71–73). Marx justified this tabooing with the fact that nonhuman living beings are fundamentally different from humans and thus are not considered as genus or community (Mütherich, 102). Rather, they are production materials for human labor. This view coincides with Marx's concept of nature and makes clear that nature and animals were understood as something 'utilizable.' This ultimately necessitated the perpetuation of a dichotomy between humans as subjects and animals as objects. By attributing animals as part of nature, this dichotomy continued to exist in the course of critical theory by Horkheimer and Adorno (Mütherich 2004, 125; Chimaira Arbeitskreis 2011, 18).

Although representatives of the Frankfurt School showed a more critical view on human-animal relations later on, more in-depth sociological analyses of social human-animal relations remained a desideratum. In addition, the construct of nature and its social dimensions was hardly considered in sociology. Although Durkheim and Weber do show indications of the significance of nature, these are disregarded in favor of an extra-societal view of nature (Mütherich 2004, 166–168; Sebastian 2017) and substantiated by debates in the following environmental sociology. This sociology was formed in the 1970s and dealt initially with environmental destruction and later with the correlations to capitalism, prosperity, and sustainability research (Kaldewey 2008, 2789; Lange 2011; Dunlap 2011; Bell 2012). Due to the insights gained, it was stated that a return to realism was necessary, since nature could no longer be perceived only as a social construction (Catton 1972, 437). This view led, for example, to the criticism of Luhmann's systems theory (1984, 245). This theory describes a distinction between living (humans and animals), psychological (consciousness) and social systems, and the environment surrounding them. It assumes a reality continuum of the world in which everything that exists takes on the forms of being or the form of visible and invisible things (Kaldewey 2011, 284).

This view received criticism in the environmental sociological debate. Both Hebel and Kaldewey assume, however, that the criticism of Luhmann resulted from an erroneous reception of his theory in the environmental sociological debate (Kaldewey 2008, 2827; Hebel 2003, 117). Thus, Kaldewey points out that Luhmann (1995) understands the concept of environment and nature as a model that "integrates several concepts of reality and world in itself, and (. . .) can be understood as a reconceptualization of the classical distinction between nature and society" (Luhmann, 2830). The outside world is not conceived in an absolute but in a system-relative way (Luhmann 1984, 249), which means that it is linked to the system and exists only for the system (Kaldewey 2011, 284). Kaldewey illustrates this with an example: Action is characterized by social and nonsocial structures. If nature is excluded from structure, this automatically means an inclusion in culture (Kaldewey, 294). Especially in later publications, Luhmann referred explicitly to this point. Thus, nature can by no means be described as 'outside,' since an exclusion simultaneously implies an inclusion. Only by naming something as excluded does it become semiotically real and thus included (Kaldewey 2008, 2830). Hence, Luhmann states:

> If one starts from the distinction system/environment, one must assign humans, as living and consciously experiencing beings, either to the system or to the environment. (. . .) If one were to regard humans as part of the social system, this would force one to apply the theory of differentiation as a theory of the distribution of humans—be it into social classes, be it into nations, ethnicities, groups. This would, however, lead to a blatant contradiction to the concept of human rights, especially to the concept of equality. Such a "humanism" would thus fail because of one's own ideas. All that remains is the possibility of considering the human being fully, body and soul, part of the environment of the social system. (Luhmann 1997, 29–30)

It is not surprising, therefore, that excluding animals and nature from sociological theories and empirical research processes is no longer considered contemporary.

Animals in particular are to be understood as acting actors within social processes (Wiedenmann 2009, 68). In the context of social interactions in recent debates, the analysis of precisely these human-animal relationships is based on the theoretical concept of the "Du-Evidenz" (You-Evidence) according to Geiger (1931, 283–285). This concept enables us to understand animals as equal partners and, thus, loosens the previously described dichotomy between humans and animals (Hastedt 2011, 210–211) by clarifying that the construction of animals can be changed (Wiedenmann 2009, 28). This view is supported by an analysis of Buschka and Rouamba, who examined a construction of animals by attributing a mind. This showed that the construction of animals is socially imposed. Humans construct themselves through animals (Buschka and Rouamba 2013, 28), since they occupy a substantial part of our social environment (Smith-Harris 2003, 86). Hence, the constructions of animals range from their role as hunting objects or hunting assistants to aliment to equal partners (Vernooij and Schneider 2013; Hamilton and Taylor 2013; Alger and Alger 2003, 1). The construction is closely linked to the values and judgments of animal owners or people who handle animals. They are appropriated in the course of a biography or in the course of dealing with animals (Smith-Harris 2003, 86).

A look at the current environmental sociological debate confirms this viewpoint: In early environmental sociological analyses of human-nature relationships, human society was still understood as a biocoenosis. The approach of empirical analysis of the material and energetic exchange process between society, technology, nature, and animals, which aims to obtain indications of consumption, production, settlement, and transport structures, is based on this understanding (Brand 2014, 28). At present, the relationship between society, nature, and animals is constructed by the society and is hardly characterized by nature or the animals themselves (Brand 2014, 14–15). This may be due to the fact that the duality between humans and nature or humans and animals has only been softened in recent environmental and risk debates and allows an analysis of the manifold interdependencies (Brand 2014, 19–20). Especially in recent years, this has shown that a demarcation between society and nature, which animals are rated among, is no longer sustainable (Brand 2014; Kurth et al. 2016).

The ambivalence in the various constructions of animal creatures in human-animal relationships, but also in human-nature relationships, can be explained in reference to Berger and Luckmann: The (everyday) knowledge about animals and nature and the reality of dealing with them is characterized in different ways depending on the setting. The two authors see the difference between humans and animals primarily in the fact that animals are much more geographically bound than humans.

Human beings, on the other hand, do not follow a specific environment to which they must adapt. Rather, humans developed in an interrelation with the environment through social and cultural socialization. This is particularly important for the views on nature and animals, since role assignments to animals and nature are internalized by humans and accepted as natural in the context of the relationship (Berger and Luckmann 1980, 48–52). Nature is understood here as something that has the 'upper hand.' Man's attempt to change nature and to see it as objective ultimately has an effect on society. Berger and Luckmann illustrate this with the example of hunting: Hunting takes place in the social world, which is characterized by a knowledge of hunting and a control over the act of hunting as a whole. By means of language, the acquired experience during hunting is passed on through generations. Experience as an important sign system of the social world ultimately leads to new discoveries and experiences in hunting, which again lead to a new objectivity (the more-than-human world) (Berger and Luckmann, 64–70).[1]

Although Berger and Luckmann make no direct reference to the social relationship between humans, nature, and animals, their theoretical concept allows us to draw conclusions about this relationship: The example of animal's statuses in different cultures shows that some animals are considered food in one culture, while worshiped as sacred beings in another culture. Both constructions describe an objective reality of what is considered edible and nonedible. In addition, social norms institutionalize this objectivity (Berger and Luckmann, 86–88).

In Germany, for example, the slaughtering of a dog, according to the animal protection law, would have legal consequences, whereas the slaughtering of a pig is socially and legally legitimized (Lorz and Metzger 2016, 63; Binder 2007, 809–811).

In the next step, the objective realities lead to a differentiation into subsensory worlds, which are linked to processes of institutionalization and are accompanied by processes of dissolution of collective knowledge. The emergence of subsensory worlds that are supported only by parts of society is a consequence of institutional diversification and economic affluence. Subsensory worlds open up a diverse perspective on the actions of society as a whole and, through specific knowledge, can lead to a detachment from the original social origins. In this way, subsensory worlds can develop independently and decouple themselves from the rest of the world, creating "hermetically sealed enclaves" (Berger and Luckmann 1980, 93). At this point, the problem of legitimization by society arises. Legitimization of institutions only occurs when the institution is fundamentally questioned. It must be taken into account that people often regard both the institution and its meaning as objectively given (Berger and Luckmann, 93). An emerging doubt is one of the first steps toward a "primary objectification of meaning," that is, an objectively appearing world of meaning followed by a secondary objectification. This leads to the legitimation of an institution within the institutional order of society, in which the context of meaning between existing institutions is established (Berger and Luckmann, 93).

Subsensory worlds in the context of human-animal relations are, for example, the animal protection or animal rights movement, vegetarianism, or veganism. What they all have in common is that they have a different perspective on social human-animal/human-nature relationships and that, through a legitimization by institutions, this perspective can lead to a new social legitimization. This results in an attribution of what, for example, characterizes an animal in the narrower sense and how it is characterized by structures of meaning and sense of a society (Berger and Luckmann, 93).

The outside world described by Berger and Luckmann as the "supreme reality" (93), on the other hand, is classified by Schütz as a classical everyday world and defined as a social reality.

> I understand the term 'social reality' as the totality of objects and phenomena in the social cultural world, according to the everyday understanding of people, who act in it in manifold relationships with their fellow human beings. It is the world of cultural objects and social institutions into which we are all born, in which we find our way and with which we have to deal. From the outset, we are actors in social situations and experience the world in which we live as a world of nature and culture, not as a private world, but as an intersubjective world, that is, a world common to all of us, which is either actually given or potentially experienced by everyone. (Schütz 1971, 60–61)

Within this everyday world, relationships take place between humans, nature, and animals that have not yet been sufficiently analyzed sociologically. Kaldewey attributes this to the fact that the description of a construction of nature and animals is characterized as "extra-social" (2008, 2828). A deeper look, however, shows their social category and, in the next step, leads to a doubt concerning whether beyond the social constructions of nature and animals, there actually are no further objective and natural facts.

In the sense of Durkheim and Weber, this means to perceive nature as real and not as a social reality (Kaldewey, 2828). This means that "the scientific knowledge about nature or the system-theoretical thesis of the structural coupling of the operations of social systems with their reality-substructure (. . .) can easily be understood as valid scientific knowledge about extra-social reality" (Kaldewey 2011, 304). Thus, 'real' and 'constructed' can coexist, mixing the reality of social knowledge with extra-social facts and forming the basis of a multispecies research.

Referring to Katharina Block, it can also be assumed that a natural or social environment can be equated with nature. The author derives this in reference to Plessner (1950, 1953, 1946), Rosa (2014), and von Uexküll (1964). She assumes that animals, plants, and humans exist as levels and that humans perceive their environment as a world within these levels (Block 2016, 17). This means a transformation of the concept of the environment into a concept of the world, which overcomes the constructivist and realistic conflict and promotes an interweaving of humans, nature, and culture into a "self-world *relationship*" (Block 2016, 17, emphasis added). This further development from environment to world is highly relevant both in multispecies research and in Multispecies Ethnography, whereby the differences of social-natural conditions must not remain undetermined (Becker 2016, 443–445), since system and environment can irritate each other (Kaldewey 2011, 280).

2.2 HUMANS, ANIMALS, AND NATURE IN EDUCATION

The significance of nature and animals in educational contexts is particularly relevant against the background of current developments. The multiple crises of our time require a focus on sustainable and inclusive education (Howard et al. 2019, 1). The German Commission for UNESCO is pushing for education for sustainable development to be anchored in all areas of education (German UNESCO Commission, n.d.). At the same time, it is calling for a reform of educational plans that adapts competencies and forms of instruction to global (environmental) world changes (de Haan 2012b, 37; Howard et al. 2019, 1; Jickling et al. 2018, 6).

These demands began in the 1970s, when it became clear that environmental resources would no longer be sufficient in the long term. The importance of environmental education came into focus and was incorporated into the curricula of all types of schools (Kahlert 2005, 431). Concurrently, global learning evolved to be a pillar of development policy (Maack 2018, 10; Kahlert 2005, 431; de Haan 2012a). The key objective of sustainable and environmentally sound development, which was recognized worldwide in 1987 (Hauff 1987, 51), influenced both the pillar of global learning and that of environmental education. In the 1990s, both pillars finally led to the concept of Education for Sustainable Development, which from then on focused on application-oriented learning (de Haan 1999, 265–267; 2002, 81–83).

Kopnina criticizes in this context the decades-long separation of environment, sustainability, health, peace, democracy, and social justice as well as the lagging adoption of the Sustainable Development Goals (SDG's) in 2015. Although the aforementioned fields are now being interlinked, this interlinking is currently only to be understood as a motor for advancing sustainable environmental education. The dovetailing of existing educational dimensions, such as peace education, human rights education, intercultural education, population education, international development education, media education, or inclusion, is fundamental to creating responsible societies (Kopnina 2017, 130–132; Sauvé 1996, 28). In this context, it must be taken into account that there are currently different approaches to the implementation of sustainable environmental education projects framed by organizations, stakeholders, and teachers (Sauvé 1996, 28; Grund and Brock 2018; Brock and Grund 2018; Maack 2018).[2] In addition, despite the UN Decade, there has been no "implementation in the structures and everyday life of the education system" (de Haan 2015, 16).

A similar picture is painted both by the analyses of the stabilization of environmental education (Gräsel 2002, 681–683; Leeming et al. 1993; Kahlert 2005, 433; Lob 1997, 201; Lehmann 1999; Krumm 1996) and by an analysis of the implementation of the goals of sustainable development. No country in the group of Organisation for Economic Co-operation and Development (OECD) countries will achieve all 17 Sustainable Development Goals (SDGs) by 2030 (Bertelsmann Foundation and SDSN 2018, 13).

The national and international discourses, which are conducted in the context of sustainable education, illustrate a consensus among scientists that nature and animals must be more strongly included in educational processes in the future (Jickling et al. 2018; Howard et al. 2019; Zivkovic 2017; Morgen 2017; Kopnina 2017; Ameli and Hühn 2016). This requires a reform of educational plans and teaching methods to include nature and animals and to adapt the learning goals and content to local and global (environmental) world changes (de Haan 2012b, 37; Howard et al. 2019, 1; Sauvé 1996, 7–9). This means a shift toward new transformative educational paradigms, which include a reflection of contemporary worldviews (O'Brien and Howard 2016, 128; Coles et al. 2017; Wals et al. 2017). In doing so, the attention is on human beings, animals, and nature in the context of their individual work. And, more than ever, there is a focus on interdisciplinary education, which concentrates on competencies of content knowledge, methodological knowledge, knowledge application, and effective collaboration (Brundiers and Wiek 2011). This includes critical thinking, communication with the more-than-human world, networking, creativity, problem-solving skills, personality development, and political education (Howard et al. 2019, 4).

In this context, Sauvé states—with reference to Environmental and Sustainable Education—the necessity of questioning the typology of the conception of nature and the significance of environmental education linked to it. The environment, which he equates with nature, requires appreciation, respect, and protection. At the same time, it must be made clear that nature as a resource requires problem-solving-oriented management. This is linked to the certainty that humans are part of this environment and (co-)responsible for it (Sauvé 1996, 10–12).

Kopnina (2017) proposes a similar approach: She calls for an overcoming of anthropocentrism in education in order to reorient it toward nature and nonhumans. For this purpose, she proposes a planetary citizenship so that all species have the right to a sustainable life of their own (Kopnina, 137). This means that "environmental compatibility (. . .) requires both practical and ethical commitment on behalf of non-humans" (Kopnina, 130). This results in (new) perspectives from different disciplines and a transdisciplinary integration of nonacademic participants in the community and the multiethnic world (Valley et al. 2017, 219).

The inclusion of the more-than-human world in education and research in various disciplines is relevant to sustainable environmental education in all school and extracurricular educational contexts. Furthermore, the importance of reflexivity and critical thinking as a relevant component in teaching and learning situations is elementary. To this end, educators in various regions (of the world) should be seen as an important source for transformative sustainable environmental education (Wals et al. 2017, 27; Valley et al. 2017, 218; Rees 2003, 93), because only together can current educational systems be reconsidered. A solid foundation can only be built by pursuing and consolidating the goals of sustainable environmental education and professionally integrating nature and animals into all learning environments (Selby and Kagawa 2015; Raus and Falkenberg 2015).

According to Gebhard (2013), the inclusion of nature and animals is also relevant for the psychological development of children and young people. Rousseau already emphasized that in addition to things, humans need nature as an educator (Rousseau 1978, 10). "Nature develops our abilities and our powers; humans teach us how to use these abilities and powers. But things educate us by the experience we have with them and by the way we see them" (Rousseau 1978, 10). Especially in the second phase of childhood, the more-than-human world plays a major role (Rousseau, 63). Children need access to the living environment such as meadows, fields, bushes, forests, and watering places (Otterstädt 1962, 278) in order to acquire knowledge with and about nature (Leontjev 1973, 233). This acquisition usually takes place on an unconscious level (Gebhard 2013, 18), although children do not proceed rudely in this respect. Rather, studies show that their interaction is generally gentle and caring in experimenting and exploring nature (Hart 1979, 1982; Gebhard 2013, 78). From a psychological point of view, the 'outer' nature always influences the inner, psychological environment of humans and supports the use of symbols as patterns of interpretation in order to form identities (Gebhard, 38).

However, nature is not only described as something elementary in children. Adults also show an emotional orientation toward 'real' nature. This serves as an island in the fast-moving circumstances of life, without dismissing one's own human identity (Gebhard 2013, 27). Adults therefore often associate a feeling of freedom with nature (Gebhard, 85), which however requires that real 'facts of nature' are no longer perceived and described as such (Pschera 2014, 41–43). This lack of access to nature and animals results not least from a focus on aesthetics. The aesthetic focus is something that is increasingly found in adults, while children understand contact with nature more as a leisure activity, although aesthetics also plays a role here (Gebhard 2013, 102).

Various theories show the interrelationships of these mentioned aspects in contact with the living environment. For example, psychological and neurobiological research assumes that humans, and especially children, need the environment (Gebhard 2013, 74; Hüther 2005, 2008). Another approach that describes human contact with nature as something elementary is the controversial biophilia hypothesis. This hypothesis assumes that people must have contact with the nature surrounding them, since the physical, cognitive, and emotional orientation toward living nature is a basic human need (Wilson 1984, 1–2; Kellert and Wilson 1993, 3). This can be supported by empirical results. For example, studies show that nature plays an important role for children between the ages of 6 and 15 (Brämer 2006; Gmeiner 2003), since closeness to nature is particularly relevant to the development of consciousness and the sense of dynamic developments in this phase (Gebhard 2013, 82). However, direct contact with nature decreases the more electronic media are available in the household in which the children live (Brämer 2006; Gmeiner 2003). The trend toward electronic media has become more stable in recent years, with the result that nature now plays a subordinate role in the leisure activities of children and young people. However, this is attributed to not only media consumption but also to the regimentation by nature, as young people in particular complain about a lack of opportunity to shape nature and can no longer identify with it (Gebhard 2013, 75).

Nevertheless, these findings show "a remarkable contradiction: On the one hand, nature activities (. . .) are considered unattractive, on the other hand, nature areas (. . .) are visited to a considerable extent" (Gebhard, 75).[3] Anxious feelings also occupy a space within the experience of nature and can serve to relativize a romanticizing of the human-nature connection (Gebhard 2013, 87–88). However, the fear here does not generally result from nature itself, but derives, for example, from loneliness or darkness (Hallmann et al. 2005).

Although numerous results—on how education interacts with nature—have been published, a look at the current study situation shows that it is not conclusively and uniformly clarified how nature and animals must be integrated into educational processes. Although there are already a variety of concepts that focus on nature- and animal-based learning (Vernooij and Schneider 2013; Ameli et al. 2016; Sempik et al. 2010, 28; Humberstone et al. 2016), these

often vary in their definition approaches. The example of two countries—
Germany and Canada—will be used to illustrate differences and similarities in
the understanding of interactions between humans, nature and animals in educational processes: The German approach to nature and animals in education
follows a differentiated exclusion. While the concept of nature-based intervention has hardly become established, the professional field of animal-based services (with a reference to nature) comprises a great deal of differentiation. In
Germany, animal-supported services in school and out-of-school educational
organizations are very often located under the umbrella of animal-supported
therapy (Ameli 2016, 42–44). LaJoie was able to show that 20 different
definitions and 12 different job titles are used for the form of intervention of
animal-assisted therapy alone (LaJoie 2003, quoted from Kruger and Serpell
2006, 22–23). In addition, further established terms are named, such as nature
education, farm pedagogy, garden therapy, or the differentiation, according to
the animal species used, such as dog-supported pedagogy in schools or horse-
supported coaching in adult education (Ameli et al. 2016; Gebhard 2013, 108;
Haubenhofer and Strunz 2013).

In Germany, animal-based services in the form of therapy, education, and
support measures are usually characterized as human-(house-)animal interactions (Vernooij and Schneider 2013), while in Canada, they are generally
described as "wildlife-human interactions" (Bath and Enck 2003, 4–6; Sorge
2008, 180). The latter imply that the interactions between students, nature,
and wildlife, such as birds, reptiles, and insects, influence students beyond
learning and require a positive attitude and critical engagement with animals
and nature (Sorge 2008, 180; Peternell 2014, 24–26). The Canadian concept
shows close parallels to the 'Green Care' concept. This concept combines
all nature- and animal-based interactions under one term, even though its
orientation shows a stronger tendency toward therapeutic than educational
approaches (Sempik et al. 2010, 28; Humberstone et al. 2016). Moreover, the
Canadian concept does not draw a strict line between nature and animals in
educational processes, but rather connects both areas through indigenous perspectives[4] on nature and animals in teaching/learning processes (Henderson
and Potter 2001, 231–233). Living Schools or the Living Campus can be
cited as examples of this (Howard et al. 2019; O'Brien and Adam 2016).[5]
The interactions of humans, animals, and nature in Canada will be integrated
as part of the 'Nature and Public Health' strategy (van den Bosch and Bird
2018) into an overall concept that takes into account the complexity and
dynamics of biological, material, social, and cultural dimensions (van den
Bosch and Bird, 3).

Common to the German and Canadian nature- and animal-based educational processes is that both nature and nature- and animal-based education are
taught and learned (Henderson and Potter 2001, 231–233; Ameli et al. 2016;

Haubenhofer and Strunz 2013). The importance of this form of teaching / learning is based on the finding that the direct and active contact of pupils and students with animals and nature has a lasting effect on their interaction with them (Nicoll et al. 2008; Gebhard 2013, 118–122). The assumption that teaching / learning processes are closely interwoven with nature and animals, and have a significant influence on sustainable lifestyles and require "well-being for all" is linked to this (O'Brien and Howard 2016, 118).

This assumption can be partially supported by empirical findings in the context of nature experience and environmental awareness. For example, Hallmann et al. (2005) showed a positive correlation between the stay in nature and the subjective view of nature conservation (Gebhard 2013, 117), which could be confirmed by further research (Lude 2001, 2006; Bögeholz 1999, 22). These results are not only applicable to free interactions, but are also recognizable for pedagogically initiated experiences of nature (Gebhard 2013, 118–122). Furthermore, effects of interactions with nature and animals for psychological and physiological parameters are described and regarded health-promoting. Thus, Searles describes that the relationship to living nature can bring about an alleviation of pain and anxiety-stricken emotional states. The deepening of the sense of reality can lead to a promotion of the own personality and appreciation of the own self, as well as a positive attitude toward fellow human beings. In addition, contact with animate nature can have an influence on concentration, a reduction in aggression potential or stress-relieving effects (Searles 1960, 122; Jutras 2003; Taylor et al. 2001). Similar effects are described for animal-based services. Here, different types of effects can be seen on the physical, psychological, and social levels (Hohmann 2012, 49).

Although there are already many different terms and a deeper differentiation of the field has taken place (Ameli 2016), in view of the global significance of nature- and animal-supported education, an umbrella term should be established, under which all nature- and animal-supported educational processes with all their concepts can be united and new concepts are made possible. The term 'multispecies education' is proposed for this purpose.

Multispecies Education

The choice of this term is based on the idea of a concept that implements a nature- and animal-based teaching and learning with relevant areas. The concept thus represents an extension of existing concepts and at the same time a transformation, since it follows a holistic educational approach. This requires that humans and the surrounding animate and inanimate environment, i.e. animals, plants, and other living creatures, are actively included in educational processes (Wals et al. 2017, 19–21). In doing so, not only the human agency but also the agency of animate and inanimate nature, as well as animals, will be considered.[6] The methodology of Multispecies Ethnography serves as a bridge between the disciplines and helps practice teaching in networks. This is always independent of the educational environment, because Multispecies Ethnography can be used in all subjects and allows for observation in HumansAnimalsNaturesCultures.

Multispecies education describes a process of passive education toward an active education of and with nature and animals and follows an integrative thinking of all actors in a sustainable network. The inclusion of animals and the more-than-human world through a multiplicity of species connects areas of scientific qualitative research with observations of daily life. In doing so, a reflexivity arises from observations and active contact with nature and animals. The inclusion of students enables transformative learning, so that Multispecies Ethnography offers the possibility of a research method and an educational method for all age groups at the same time (Hamilton and Taylor 2017, 136).

The participation of animals and a near-natural environment in terms of sustainable environmental education currently raises questions. For example, the significance, role allocation, and social construction of nature and animals within educational settings have not yet been conclusively analyzed. In addition, it has not been conclusively clarified on a theoretical and practical level how the more-than-human world is used within teaching-learning processes and how the consideration of the agency is implemented concretely. The discussion about competencies in the context of teacher training at universities and schools is currently moving into focus (Wiek et al. 2011, 129; Barth et al. 2007, 419; Coles et al. 2017, 77–78; Raus and Värri 2017, 104; Morgan 2017, 120 ff; Barraza and Ruiz-Mallén 2017, 262). The lack of consideration of the agency of animals and nature in these educational contexts makes it clear that, in addition to the aspect of the concrete inclusion of nature and animals, this must be placed even more strongly in the focus of future research.

2.3 HUMANS, ANIMALS, AND NATURE IN THE NATURAL SCIENCES

For a long time, a relationship between humans and nature was taken for granted, even though this was masked for a long time by the Christian religion as well as the natural sciences (Gerhard 2013, 19). The understanding of nature in scientific disciplines shows that nature is understood as 'all living things.' This includes humans and the animate and inanimate nature surrounding him; that is, water, soil, and air as well as stones, trees, or animals (Michel-Fabian 2010, 47).

In 2000, Paul Crutzen called for the introduction of a new geological epoch, the Anthropocene, and since then it has been discussed in scientific disciplines (Haraway 2018, 67; Subcommission on Quaternary Stratigraphy 2016; Crutzen and Stoermer 2000). It follows the Holocene, in which nature was considered much more strongly as something almighty (Haraway 2018, 67). The focus on a new geological age results from the assumption that, firstly, the influences of human activity have been proven to have transformative effects on the Earth and, secondly, geopolitical foundations have been destroyed (Crutzen and Stoemer 2000; Crutzen 2000). As a result, nature has become more than ever a human concern, although the final decision on whether the Anthropocene will replace the Holocene is still pending (Springer 2016; Subcommission on Quaternary Stratigraphy 2016). In addition to the discussed effects of humans on the environment, increasing digitization makes it necessary to analyze how the collectives of the world are connected (Latour 2017).

The debates conducted in this context can be seen as a foundation for future orientation in multispecies research, although scientific research shows that it focuses on "characteristic features of knowledge acquisition and the properties of scientific knowledge" (Kremer 2010, 8). In this context, questions are formulated in a hypothesis-led manner and tested by means of observations, comparisons, and experiments in order to increase the significance of the models (Wellnitz and Mayer 2008, 136–137). The following understanding in the analysis and interpretation of the models is described as scientific thinking and includes an interpretation of the observations made. At its core, this procedure follows an understanding of nature that is based on evidence of real events (Kremer 2010, 9–11).[7]

In principle, the logic of research differs only rudimentarily from that of the natural and social sciences, since both disciplines record the respective "objects through direct observation or indirectly via indicators, and for both, scientific progress consists on the one hand of discovering previously unknown phenomena or describing known ones more precisely" (Mayntz 2005, 5). Ultimately, various research techniques also play a decisive role in the acquisition of scientific knowledge. This illustrates a connection between research technology and research logic. In contrast to the social sciences, scientific research increasingly uses powerful instruments for observation, measurement, and experimental manipulation to classify information as part of the whole. As in the social sciences, for example, the focus here is on statistical, mathematical, and computer-based methods of analysis and observations (Mayntz, 6–8).

The special execution of observations in the natural sciences describes a complex and attention-guided method of cognition, which follows certain criteria. It involves systematic planning, direct or indirect observation, counting, describing, and writing down, with simultaneous questioning (Sturm 1974; Wellnitz and Mayer 2008, 135; Mahner and Bunge 2000). The scientific approach linked to this is characterized by a hypothetical-deductive research method and thus requires repeated checking and control of the collected data. In this way, the quality criteria, validity, reliability, and accuracy of the data are met in order to establish generally applicable rules (Randler 2018, 19–21; Wellnitz and Mayer 2008, 135). Lorimer and Driessen, from the discipline of environmental sciences and geography, describe the procedure of two models of experiments, which are illustrated in table 2.1.

While the classical experiment is characterized as a laboratory situation that depicts the order of nature to society, 'wild experiments'—named by the authors—focus on a microscopic view of humans and nonhumans in their places. Wild Experiments follows less a hypothetical-deductive than an open and unbiased method design (Lorimer and Driessen 2017, 110).

'Wild experiments' in scientific research are particularly interesting before the understanding of biomedical and biological research. Although the orientation of so-called 'wild experiments' is of elementary importance for future multispecies research, it can be assumed that this paradigm shift will cause some hurdles for some scientific disciplines, but that researchers are willing to face these hurdles. This can be illustrated by the diversity of approaches: Experiments in laboratories allow scientists to control the object under investigation (Gieryn 2006, 5). Technically and culturally delimited spaces provide knowledge (Lorimer and Driessen 2017, 107) and shield disturbances of the openness (Gieryn 2006, 6). In this way, analysis for human conditions is particularly emphasized, while wild experiments refer much more strongly—for example in primatology—to a research relationship between humans and animals (Shah 2020, 423). This approach is also demonstrated by the example of Jane Godall. Although she pointed out that great apes have emotions, her

Table 2.1 Key Properties of Research Models

	Experiment	*Wild Experiment*
Ontology	Transcendent order of nature and society	Immanent and indefinite world of humans and nonhumans of the more-than-human world
Epistemology	Hypothetico-deductive method	Open approach, designed to create surprises
Politics	Delegating: Science provides facts; politics decide what counts	Dialogical: Knowledge is generated and negotiated in emerging collectives
Placing	The laboratory (and more rarely 'the field')	The 'wild' in the real more-than-human world

Source: Own representation in accordance with Lorimer and Driessen (2017, 110).

reports were initially ridiculed. She was only able to gain acceptance for her results after she was able to substantiate her findings with statistics and thus achieve a reputation for her contributions (Hamilton and Taylor 2017, 61). Donna Haraway points to similar findings with van Dooren and Despret (2018), who analyzed the emotions of Hawaiian crows and found that they have an ability to mourn. However, acceptance of the results will only come about through ethological proof of research of this kind in the scientific community (Haraway 2018, 58; Panksepp 2005; Paul and Mendl 2018).

Ethology as a subarea of scientific research is of particular relevance to multispecies research, since it explicitly studies the behavior of different species and thus, not least, records influences on the psychological discipline (Ellgring 1984, 211). Based on biological methods, ethology analyzes the behavior of various animal and human beings with regard to their physiological, ontogenetic, and evolutionary perspectives. Sociobiology, as a branch of ethology, also focuses on the interrelationships between species and their surrounding animate and inanimate environment (Ellgring, 211). Darwin provided an important basis for modern evolutionary biology by making observations of individual cases without conducting controlled experiments (Irvine 2004, 66; Kappeler 2017, 9). With George Romanes, Charles Whitman, and Oskar Heinroth, further foundations for the zoology and the psychology were laid. In the further course of Behaviorism (Kappeler 2017, 9–11) and the following 20th century, classical ethology was established through the method of the ethogram and almost solidified by the work of Konrad Lorenz, Karl von Frisch and Nikolaas Tinbergen. These foundations still serve today as a foundation for the established subdisciplines of modern ethology—behavioral ecology, sociobiology, and behavioral research (Kappeler, 12–14).

In the further course of time, the ethological results were able to further develop the methodological diversity. Thus, in addition to phylogenetic and ontogenetic considerations, ethograms or cultural comparisons currently exist in ethological research (Ellgring 1984, 213). It is striking that, similar to the social science research method, the investigations are characterized by direct field access and, in addition, "paper and pencil" are described as elementary instruments (Kappeler 2017, 20). At present, however, a trend toward tracking programs or transponders is emerging due to digitization (Lennox et al. 2017; Muhametsafina et al. 2014; McConell et al. 2016; Luschi and Casale 2014).[8]

Despret (2004) points out for ethological research in the form of behavioral observations the special importance of the own body for research in the field.[9] This aspect appears as a relevant variable but is largely ignored in the ethological literature (Kappeler 2017, 20–22; Ellgring 1984, 211–213; Randler 2018, 19–21). Despret therefore uses the example of an analysis of human-animal interactions in hunters and cattle breeders to clarify this aspect for ethological research: A hunter follows the animals into their own field and observes them there. A cattle breeder, on the other hand, keeps them with him to offer them what he considers to be the natural environment, and to make the observations there. Both field approaches have in common that they are always characterized by the introduction of the own body and thus significantly influence planned experiments and observations (Despret 2004, 130). A well-known example is the 'Clever Hans Effect.' Before World War I, the Clever Hans, together with his trainer, attracted the attention of a wider public. The Orlov Trotter was apparently able to solve mathematical problems by tapping with his hoof or nodding. Von Osten, the horse's trainer, attempted to prove that horses are capable of solving arithmetical problems if they are taught how to with the right didactic method. Analysis by a scientific commission showed that the horse reacted to the finest nuances of the body language and facial expressions of its owner or the audience. This allowed the horse to know when to stop tapping with its hoof. This shows that the body and body language of the 'experimenter' had a high significance for the reaction of the horse (Hans). The ethological analysis thus allowed the realization that the use of the body caused the experiment to be influenced. It could hence be shown that this leads to misinterpretation of animal behavior by human analyses because they interpret other living beings from their human logic (Samhita and Gross 2013; Stamp Dawkins 2007).

Despret sees in it, nevertheless, the confirmation of a kind of relationship confirmed, since humans are given the possibility to be like a horse and horses are given the possibility to be like a human. This leads on both sides to adaptable articulations, which, in turn, open up the possibility of communicating differently (with each other) (Despret 2004, 130).

According to Fehrle et al., the aforementioned developments in the perception of animals mean that in the future, evolutionary-, behavioral-, and neuro-research in particular can hardly be viewed in isolation from social and ethical issues (Fehrle et al. 2010, xi). This is not a matter of drawing a development of the entities from 'hard' natural science to 'soft' humanities. Rather, the aim is to make the boundaries between the disciplines more permeable in the future, both to raise the profile of all disciplines and to offer opportunities to solve problems that can be better solved collaboratively than alone (Fehrle et al., xvi). Although the authors emphasize the importance of this interdisciplinarity, they also point out the relevant differences in the individual disciplines. In some cases, these differences create a feeling of "inferior knowledge" (Fehrle et al., xvi) among representatives of different disciplines, which prevents them from working together. This requires an openness to overcome this hurdle (Fehrle et al., xvi).

2.4 HUMANS, ANIMALS, AND NATURE
IN VETERINARY MEDICINE

In hardly any other discipline, do animals play such an important role, in comparison to nature, as in veterinary medicine. Animal protection, the treatment of sick animals, and laboratory animal science describe relevant areas of the veterinary profession, whose research is based on the principles of the methods of human medicine, biology, and zoology.

At the beginning of the 18th century, the developing profession of veterinarians was strongly professionalized in the treatment of animal diseases, the fight against animal epidemics and the expert evaluation of meat quality (Schauder 1957, 100–101; 108–109). In addition to the differentiation of the mentioned fields of activity in the further course of the 19th century, the field of veterinary drug research was added (Gebhard, 103). From the middle of the 19th century onward, laboratory animal science also played a decisive role in the veterinary profession (GV-SOLAS 2013).[10]

In recent years, the existing structures of the veterinary profession are questioned both on a societal level and in (inter-)disciplinary dialogues (Taylor et al. 2008; Dilly and Tipold 2014, 1). This results from the fact that the veterinary medical discipline is confronted with a multitude of 'real social problems' that require an openness to overcome disciplinary boundaries (Hamilton and Taylor 2017, 65). This leads to a reflection not only on existing veterinary education but also on the inclusion of animals in biomedical scientific research (Dilly and Tipold 2014, 1; Johnson and Degeling 2012, 45–47). This development has led to the introduction of so-called skills labs in veterinary education (Dilly and Tipold 2014) and the assumption that animals are assigned an "animal capital"[11] (Irvine 2004, 66–67). In addition, the demand arose that the status of patients must be attributed to animals within experiments. This is to give greater consideration to animal agency in order to practice readjustment with respect to animal welfare (Johnson and Degeling 2012, 45–47).

In biomedical research, Stephanie Krämer uses the example of the mouse as a model organism to point out its role for human cognitive interest and thus the close connection between humans and animals. She describes the reason for this as the abundance of similar genes that exist between humans and mice and lead to similar molecular processes and diseases. These similarities have led to a multitude of cognitive gains that give mice the etiquette to act as true life savers (Krämer 2019). This life-saving function is viewed extremely critically on the part of the animal protection and animal rights movement. Their influence has contributed to a changing understanding and the search for alternatives, especially in the field of laboratory animal science (Milz 2009; Blattner 2019).

Already in 1959, Russell and Burch formulated relevant parameters of a changed handling of animals in biomedical research. However, this demand did not become the focus of scientific attention until many years later and can currently be observed in efforts to establish a 3Rs strategy: The aim of the 3Rs concept is to develop replacement and alternative methods (Replace), to minimize the number of animals required for experiments to an absolute minimum (Reduce) and, where animal experiments are necessary, to reduce the number of procedures involving animals and their degree of distress in the long term (Refine) (Russell and Burch 1959; Krämer 2019).

This was first implemented with the declaration of animal protection as a national goal in 2002, followed by the anchoring of the EU Directive 2010/63, which approved the implementation of the 3R concept on the European level. In 2013, this was finally transferred to national law. Although the 3R concept is slowly establishing itself politically at European level and relevant models already exist, practice shows insufficient access to them. Even with alternative models that are superior to the mouse model, no change can be observed in everyday laboratory animal science routines (Krämer 2019).

In addition to the 3R strategy, the core idea of a symbiosis of human and animal health is combined with the consideration of relevant environmental aspects. This is based on the assumption that a healthy planet is the basis for healthy humans and healthy animals. This is currently not sufficiently linked in the public debate and from a scientific perspective.

The subsequent development began in 1984 with the idea of One Medicine, which called for medical and veterinary collaboration to combat zoonoses. In the course of time, the One Health approach developed from the One Medicine-principles and through the addition of the health of the eco-system (Schwabe 1984; Kahn et al. 2007; Zinsstag et al. 2011). This finally culminated in the framework concept 'Contributing to One World, One Health' through the World Health Organization, the Food and Agriculture Organization of the United Nations and the World Organization for Animal Health. This aims to reduce infectious diseases at the human-animal-environment interface as well as organizational links in the area of human-animal (domestic and wildlife) environment (FAO, WHO, OEI, UN System Influenza Coordination, UNICEF, The World Bank 2008; Papadopoulos and Wilmer 2011, 2–3). In the course of further development, more and more disciplines were involved in order to discuss the challenges, limits, and implementation options of the approach with representatives of various disciplines (Papadopoulos and Wilmer 2011, 2–3). The American Veterinary Medical Association thus describes One Health as "the combined effort of various disciplines, locally, nationally and globally, to achieve optimal health for humans, animals and our environment" (American Veterinary Medical Association 2008).[12]

The One Health concept responds to the growing world population, migratory movements, and environmental degradation by developing multidisciplinary measures to alleviate and prevent disease (Papadopoulos and Wilmer 2011, 1–2).[13] The harmonization of human, animal, and ecosystem health plays a role both in food safety by combating hunger and ensuring equitable resource distribution, in addressing the problem of antibiotic resistance and coping with climate change, and in poverty reduction in developing countries by reducing zoonoses (Veterinarians without Borders Vétérinaires sans Frontières—Canada 2010; Okello et al. 2011).

The importance of the One Health concept was also demonstrated at the AnimalhealthEurope Annual Conference held in 2017. There, the well-being and quality of life of humans and animals in relation to nature was discussed (Bundesverband für Tiergesundheit 2017). The concept is based on three pillars, which in principle, however, are focused on the health of animals:

1. Healthy humans: Healthy animals contribute to human health and well-being, by reducing zoonoses through medication and vaccination. This serves the food security as well as the quality preservation of food.
2. Healthy animals: Animals need medical care to ensure animal welfare and thereby increase productivity to safeguard food.
3. Healthy planet: The health of the planet is linked to healthy animals, which enable farmers to produce food with less environmental impact (AnimalHealthEurope 2017).

In addition to the relevance of One Health for One World, the concept illustrates the relevance of the cooperation between (veterinary) medical and scientific disciplines in the sense of holistic multispecies research. In its scientific understanding, the approach thus illustrates a close connection between animals, humans, and the surrounding animate and inanimate environment. It explicitly assumes that all actors have an influence on each other (Latour 2008) and that all species involved have the power to act in the 'health of the world' in order to achieve health and well-being[14] as a key objective. In this context, Huth et al. (2019, 91–93) criticize that the concept of One Health does not take a differentiated view of the framing of diseases and excludes the complex and multi-layered nature of the concept's orientation. A further point of criticism is that health is very much oriented toward a 'good' usability of animals, which in principle must be discussed in greater depth in the One Health approach.

Last but not least, a major challenge lies in implementing the approach by coordinating all the actors involved from the human, animal, and environmental spheres. Here, it has already become apparent that the interface with the environmental sciences has not yet been sufficiently strengthened

(Papadopoulos and Wilmer 2011, 4), and that cultural and social sciences have been completely ignored.

Although interdisciplinary collaboration between medicine, veterinary medicine, and environmental science is seen as an essential step, the extension of interdisciplinary collaboration to social sciences and especially educational science disciplines can be encouraged. This not only is relevant against the background of the different perspectives of these disciplines on humans, animals, and nature but also plays a major role in the continuity of the approach with regard to sustainable development from an educational science perspective.

2.5 HUMANS AND ANIMALS IN THE INTERDISCIPLINARY DIALOGUE OF HUMAN-ANIMAL STUDIES

In my dissertation (Ameli 2016), I worked out how the relationship between humans and animals has developed over time: The pronounced ambivalence in the human-animal relationship is based on the assumption of a (moral) superiority of humans over animals (Dierauer 1999, 37–38; Wils 1999, 409–410). Thus, it is assumed that humans distinguish themselves from animals through reason, language, and the ability to reflect on their own actions (Dierauer 1999, 44–45; Wils 1999, 415.). This results in the maintenance of a dichotomy, although social assignments of functions and roles to animals and the natural environment have changed (Dierauer 1999, 75–77; Nitschke 1999, 228–229; Chimaira Arbeitskreis 2011; Mütherich 2004).

As early as the Middle Ages, animals were assigned different roles (Störk 1999, 95–97), and the anthropocentric orientation in the early modern era also led to the classification of animals (Nowosadtko 1999, 255; Buchner-Fuhs 1999, 279), which, for example, focused on medical animal experiments or breeding of farm animals and animals for pleasure (Buchner-Fuhs 1999, 283; Brantz and Mauch 2010, 7). In addition, documented differences in cultural imprinting to individual preferences and culturally typical views on animals are described (Otterstedt 2009, 310–311). Indigenous peoples, for example, often have a less pronounced claim to superiority over animals, while Islamic societies generally ascribe a significantly lower status to animals than to humans (Eisenstein 1999, 121–123).

The described developments and different views on animals promoted the importance of animal protection. Through this, the Reich Animal Welfare Act could be passed in 1933 (Brand and Stöver 2008, 220), which was initially pushed back in the course of World War II by the prohibition of animal protection organizations. In the 1980s, new animal protection and animal rights movements were able to gain momentum—also due to Peter Singer and Tom Regan's call[15] for a fairer world of multispecies rights (Brand and Stöver 2008, 226; 232–234).

In the course of the developments and generation of knowledge described earlier, the development of an independent research area, human-animal studies, arose. Depending on the setting, these are also referred to as animal studies, critical animal studies, or anthrozoology (Hamilton and Taylor 2017, 7). Human-animal studies is interdisciplinary in nature and adapts research methods from the individual disciplines involved. This greatly promotes a pluralism of methods from which the disciplines of origin benefit (Kompatscher et al. 2017, 201).[16] This pluralism of methods can also be linked to Donna Haraway's metaphor of "string games." These stand for different yet interlocking paths and overlaps between disciplines (Haraway 2018, 67). It is essential to remain restless (Haraway 2018) in order to understand animals as part of society and thus also as actors within social-natural interactions. Already in 2008, Donna Haraway drew attention to the deeply intimate and contradictory relationships between humans and animals (Haraway 2008), which have not yet been conclusively reflected for natural encounters.

Human-animal studies assume that the human-animal relationship is a concrete relationship between two individuals, which are embedded as a whole in social structures. Accordingly, there is not one human-animal relationship, but rather many intersecting and interrelated human-animal relationships that are characterized by ambivalences (Buschka et al. 2012, 17). Human-animal studies already show a variety of investigations and analyses of human-animal relationships (Buschka et al. 2012; Roscher 2012; Shapiro 2008; Shapiro and DeMello 2010; Kurth et al. 2016). They comprehensively depict relationships between humans and animals and present their ambivalent views in an open-ended way. In the German-speaking world, the approach is particularly concerned with the consideration of the (historical) change in the relationship between humans and animals, the construction of animals (by humans) as well as social interactions that exist between humans and animals (Buschka et al. 2012, 23). In English-speaking countries, these research foci are complemented by the area of animal welfare (Shapiro and DeMello 2010, 307–309) and the use of animals as objects of science (Pedersen 2011a, 16). In the context of human-animal studies analyses, suitable methods for researching human-animal interactions are currently being discussed (Hamilton and Taylor 2013), in order to eliminate the exclusion of animals, which has been practiced up to now as a theoretical and methodological shortcoming in the sociological discipline (Hamilton and Taylor 2013, 176).

A comprehensive study of human-animal relationships within social processes is closely linked to the interaction of different disciplines. So, in addition to sociology, history, cultural studies, educational sciences, and psychology, biology, veterinary medicine, agricultural science, and, last but not least, law, too, play a decisive role in the analysis of human-animal relationships in particular, but also of human-nature relationships in general.

The differences in the disciplines, but also possible differences between humans and animals, lead to discussions time and again. Like the sociological discipline in more recent environmental sociological discourses, human-animal studies also assumes that the strict separation between humans, nature, and animals cannot be maintained (Brand 2014, 16; Alger and Alger 2003; Irvine 2004). Representatives of veterinary medicine, too, have recognized that cooperation in the context of the relationship between humans and animals is linked to interdisciplinary alliances (Krämer 2019).

This once again provides the opportunity to give animals the ability to act socially, to build relationships and to interact (Kurth et al. 2016, 7 ff; Alger and Alger 2003; Irvine 2004). The actions of animals can thus be related to the actions of others (individuals) (Ameli 2016, 29) and are referred to as "agency" (Kurth et al. 2016, 7–9). This agency attributes to animals an explicit power of action, which is characterized by the fact that thoughts,[17] intentions, and emotions are shared (Steinbrecher 2009, 272; Irvine 2004, 172–173).[18] Irvine concludes this from the differentiation of the concept of symbolic interactionism and works out that, regardless of language, there is a connection between humans and animals that influences their own identity (Irvine 2004, 174).

The sociologist Uwe Schimank also assumes that animals are able to act socially and to enter into relationships (Schimank 2010, 38–40). The prerequisite for this is that the interrelated behavior is linked to the existence of a social relationship and only comes about through social action (Schimank, 38). Despite his view of animals as inferior beings, Mead also makes it clear that "every living being that perceives something carries out a process of mediation within an action, and conscious mediation is an intellectual inference" (Mead 1980, 158).

Derrida states that there is a fundamental border between humans and animal and that their ignorance is an illusion. Thus, he remarks that the opposite attitude implies that the animal is not perceived for its own sake (Derrida 2002, 200). This view is also followed by Pschera, who assumes that only the recognition of otherness in the sense of an inclusive attitude can end the power over animals. Like Derida, he points out that the discussion about a possible demarcation between humans and animals is not very helpful as long as this discussion leads to a clear alienation between humans, nature and animals (Pschera 2014, 127–128; Block 2016). Only through an acceptance of differences between humans and animals and if an appreciation of these differences is practiced can change occur. This hypothesis is based on an inclusive understanding, which demands an acceptance of existing differences between humans and animals. Animals should be recognized as such, although differences in communication are visible. Thus, animals and humans communicate differently. However, this does not necessarily lead to missing interactions between humans, animals, or natural places (Pschera 2014, 127–128) The acceptance of nature and an animal in its uniqueness and differentness represents the core of the inclusive human-animal sociality and can be transferred to human-nature-animal interactions. This makes an ecology of inclusion necessary to eliminate separation and exclusion (Pschera 2014, 165; Irvine 2004, 175). Here, it is obvious that veterinary medicine, environmental sciences, and biology can provide some information about other nonhuman species, while, in return, sociology and educational science provide relevant results from society and educational processes. It is therefore elementary that nature and animal voices are heard and actively involved in (interdisciplinary) research processes.

2.6 HUMANS AND NATURES IN THE INTERDISCIPLINARY DIALOGUE OF NATURESCULTURES

While publications on the topic of human-animal studies have already become more diverse in the past 10 years, publications in the area of NaturesCultures are still underrepresented. According to Malone and Oveden (2017) and Gesing et al. (2019), the only consensus is that NaturesCultures is understood as a synthesis that recognizes an inseparability between biophysical and social relations. In its form, the concept originated from a critique of the deeply rooted dualisms between human/animal or nature/culture and finds its roots in anthropology, since it sees itself as a bridge between the disciplines (Malone and Oveden 2014, 1; Fenske 2016).

The concept of NaturesCultures goes back to Bruno Latour (1995), who in his work 'Wir waren noch nie modern' (We have never been modern, 1993) points out the inseparability of the areas contained in the term (Gesing et al. 2019, 7). NaturesCultures promotes a debate on the recognition of the branches of research at the interfaces between humans, nature, and culture. This results in behavioral and ecological interactions of a common history, which can only be identified and interpreted through a natural-cultural lens of the complex interfaces. Thus, the concept offers a multilayeredness and complexity of social-ecological relations (Malone and Oveden 2014, 2; Latour 1995, 139 f; Gesing et al. 2019, 7–9). In this context, Gesing et al. also emphasize the importance of the inclusion of all species, which as a practice are elementary for NaturesCultures (Gesing et al. 2019, 19). The research projects presented by Gesing et al. (2019) in their work "NaturesCultures" already show exemplary cross-border projects at the interface between natures and cultures, which also tie in with an "experimental turn" (Gesing et al., 26). For example, a complex ethnographic analysis of a Japanese mushroom (Tsing 2019), the analysis of the so-called wild nature in the city (Gandy 2019), or the production process of raw milk cheese in all stages of production (Paxson 2019) is presented in order to show new analytical and methodological strategies that allow for further development of research on NaturesCultures.

In addition to NaturesCultures, the approach of ethnobiology—also described as ethnoecology—can be mentioned. Ethnobiology analyzes interactions between nature and society in an interdisciplinary manner, while taking into account knowledge, technologies, and practices (Rist and Dahdouh-Guebas 2006, 476). First, ethnobiology provides concrete conceptual and methodological insights into how inter- and transdisciplinary research in the field of natural resources is structured. Second, it makes explicit norms, values, experiences, and related aspects visible in the form of specific competencies of users of natural resources in 'traditional' (e.g., farmers) and 'modern' (e.g., organic farmers) societies and analyzes their environmental knowledge.

The evaluation of nature through ethnobiological research shows how 'natural resources' are socially constructed. This results in a better understanding of the underlying principles of a steadily growing number of examples that allow highly significant contributions of local and indigenous forms of knowledge to a more sustainable use of natural resources. Third, ethnobiology contributes to making the knowledge of the local population visible in their idea of 'globality' based on their own cultural background. Fourth, it enables the creation of solid foundations for a better networking of practices, orientations, and patterns of interpretation in an intercultural perspective. Instead of competition and hegemony, the focus is on the relationship between different forms of knowledge, which are based on the respect, complementarity, and cooperation. Cultural diversity is understood here as a resource for shared knowledge and the culture-specific ontological foundations in relation to 'nature,' humans, and society and the associated relationships through which they interact are (spiritually) included (Rist and Dahdouh-Guebas, 477–479).

NOTES

1. From an animal-ethical and social point of view, hunting can also be viewed from completely different perspectives when it comes to the rights of animals and their agency in society.

2. Sustainable Environmental Education (also Environmental and Sustainable Education) is used here in line with Wals et al. (2017), as this concept combines the relevant areas of sustainable education in its roots and extends them to include nature and animal references within teaching and learning processes. This is elementary for the transformation of nature-based and animal-based education to a multispecies education as a holistic approach.

3. With regard to Margret Mead's research, it must be noted that pure nature-based education and upbringing is not enough. Using the example of the Manus, she was able to show that their children had close and varied contact with nature. However, the lack of personal attention and the development of a "basic trust" (Erikson 1968) prevented them from adequately 'using' the natural environment (Mead 1966). This shows that the interactions between caregivers and the more-than-human world are equally relevant (Gebhard 2013, 100).

4. In the context of this work, reference is made repeatedly to indigenous knowledge or indigenous perspectives. Some sources also use the term 'traditional indigenous knowledge.' In the indigenous languages, however, this would rather be translated as indigenous ways of life in nature. Whenever one of these terms is used, it is explicitly based on the ways of life in nature (Aikenhead and Michell 2011, 65). In this regard, it must be pointed out with Cajete (2006, 250) that nature in this context is described as a dynamic and flowing creation that is closely linked to our perception. Nature describes the Creative Center—translated in some cultures by colonization as Mother Earth—from which all individuals come and where they go back to. Indigenous ways of life in nature and the reality associated with them depend on the countries. Tribes and clans cannot automatically be generalized (Aikenhead and Michell 2011, 67).

5. The Living School describes a transformative educational concept, which is implemented in close connection to nature, follows a sustainable educational concept and, linked to this, strives for the goal of well-being for all (this includes humans, the animate and inanimate environment, and animals alike). The starting point is seen in the close connection of compassion between humans and the more-than-human world, as well as a networking with local and global communities (Howard et al. 2019, 1).

6. It could be discussed whether, in addition to Multispecies Ethnography, topic-centered interaction according to Cohn and Terfurth (2007) could be suitable as a (didactic) methodology for editing teaching content in all areas of education.

7. In the context of educational processes, however, it has been shown, for example, that students have not always been able to achieve the necessary understanding in scientific thinking, for example, through a pure laboratory internship, and that real events become clear (Kremer 2010, 9–11).

8. Another methodology is Citizen Science, in which laypersons serve the scientists as co-researchers. As an example, Steward et al. are used here, who developed a computer program that analyzes cognitive abilities of dogs. The special feature of this analysis is that the coresearchers complete games and tests with their dogs. Their results are entered by them into a special program and are then evaluated. Although laypersons cannot guarantee standardized procedures, it is still possible to carry out a

statistical analysis that is reliable and reflects the cognitive abilities of dogs (Steward et al. 2015). Citizen Sciences research projects are also being conducted in other disciplines (Finke 2014).

9. The so-called actor-observer hypothesis plays an important role in ethological observations of behavior. It assumes that one's own body and a cognitive bias influence the participants of an experiment (Jones and Nisbett 1972).

10. According to official statistics, more than 46.6 million animals were used for experiments worldwide in 2005 (Taylor et al. 2008).

11. Animal Capital describes a knowledge about animals to minimize their utilization (Irvine 2004, 66).

12. The consideration of interdependencies is also interesting in terms of the corona pandemic. It illustrates the interrelationships that exist in a multispecies world (Haraway 2018) between humans, animals, viruses, and so on, on one side, and animate and inanimate nature, on the other.

13. It is obvious that measures to alleviate diseases have been developed since the beginning of medicine. However, the current orientation takes a holistic approach.

14. Well-being follows a close connection of compassion between individuals of the more-than-human world and in a networking with local and global communities (Howard et al. 2019).

15. Singer argues that people are forced by their nature to reflect suffering. This is elementary to protect the interests of every individual who is affected by the actions of other individuals. It is important to focus on the fact that the interests of all individuals are equally weighted (Singer 1975, 5). This implies that animals, in the sense of Regan, are described as subjects of life, which have emotions, longings, and social abilities and are thus similar to humans. In this way, animals, plants, and the inanimate environment become inherent (Regan 1983, 283) subjects (Milbradt 2003, 72).

16. It is interesting that the theories of the sociological discipline are taken up in the debates of human-animal studies by other disciplines and made usable for the object of research (Kompatscher et al. 2017), while the sociological discipline in particular still struggles to sufficiently include animals in its own discipline (Wiedenmann 2009).

17. The question whether animals have thoughts and how they share them is particularly controversial in ethology (Kappeler 2017).

18. In human-animal studies, for example, this results from the findings that animals have the energy to move humans (e.g., in animal-based-therapy) and to touch them emotionally (Hamilton and Taylor 2017, 45–46; 57).

Chapter 3

HumansAnimalsNaturesCultures

The idea of HumansAnimalsNaturesCultures represents a further development of Bruno Latour's NaturesCultures concept, which was analyzed in more detail by Malone and Ovenden (2017) as well as Gesing et al. (2019). Although NaturesCultures already include various species, human-animal studies and NaturesCultures in HumansAnimalsNaturesCultures are linked to resolve the "nature-animal inclusion dilemma" (Pschera 2014, 126). This results in the merging of a total of four terms into a common term to reflect the interrelationships and the inseparable dimensions of the research areas linked to them. According to Gesing (2019, 8–9), the plural for human beings, animals, natures, and cultures results from Latours (1995, 139–140) recognition that nature and culture are not arbitrary and identical, but rather different. This means that there is a shift away from a universal nature and toward natures (Gesing et al. 2019, 7).

The choice of terms for HumansAnimalsNaturesCultures is virulent, as humans are (biologically) described as animals (Glock 2016), "which live in symbiosis with certain animal and plant species" (Mauss 2013, 110).

For this symbiosis, the realization that, for example, the Polynesian migration of peoples is linked to the history of plants and animals means that observers acquire a sense of individuality of each actor in the more-than-human world (in the research process). Consequently, the entire social morphology is always used to determine a target group, for example, distribution area, language, or group membership (Mauss 2013, 110). Nevertheless, with regard to the language used, it must be determined how category formation is carried out and taken up in the context of Multispecies Ethnography. The attention paid to analyses of HumansAnimalsNaturesCultures, hence, does not call existing scientific knowledge into question. Rather, the interdependencies in which they are embedded are reflected, so that categories used in the individual disciplines are included. In addition, the term in itself enables the micro-perspective view of individual actors, as well as the macro-perspective view of complex natures and cultures.

The combination of human, animal, and natural actors and their cultures should include the extended synthesis of both individual actors and their common culture. The basis of the concept is seen in the contact zones described by Donna Haraway (Haraway 2008, 8) between humans, animals, and the animate and inanimate natures, which are inseparably linked to the cultures (Malone and Ovenden 2017; Gesing et al. 2019) and which allow the analysis of highly complex interrelationships (Kropp 2015, 206–208).

Although competing and complementary views and constructions of natures, animals, humans, and cultures exist in the disciplinary considerations, there seems to be a consensus that these fields are mutually dependent and must not be viewed in isolation from one another (Bell 2012; Ameli et al. 2016; Kaldewey 2011; Krämer 2019; Subramaniam 2019). From now on, animals, which are independent actors, are not assigned to nature, as they undergo socialization and practice traditions.[1]

By referring back to indigenous knowledge, the connections between humans, animals, nature, and culture can be further substantiated. Indigenous cultures assume that culture is an essential aspect of nature, so that interdependencies and differences are depicted and analyzed in a differentiated way (Kassam 2009, 17–18). One difficulty in the analysis of culture here is its two-sided significance. On the one hand, it can mean—for the field of nature—the cultivation of plants through planting, breeding, and care. On the other hand, the same concept implies the formation of a group identity of human lifeworlds in the form of culture, which has a close connection to the environment surrounding it and refers not least to the diversity in the daily coexistence of communities (Kassam, 38).

In addition, Harmon assumes that culture represents a variety of human forms of expression and organization, which include interactions within and between the respective groups, as well as with the environment surrounding them. This includes securing one's livelihood, basis of existence, creativity, and identification with the respective group as well as a distinction from 'other' species. Two markers serve as interpretative patterns for these interactions: Biological diversity and the language for cultural diversity (Harmon 2002, 40). Culture emerges from a biological basis and integrates an inseparability of both areas, provided that the error of distinguishing languages is recognized as a significant misinterpretation (Harmon, 61–62; Harmon and Loh 2018, 660–662).

This conclusion now requires for all disciplines that humans, nature, and animals are not to be considered separately (Michel-Fabian 2010, 7). Instead, the focus has shifted to a discussion of the variability and change in the construction of nature and animals. This includes the fact that empathy and indigenous wisdom are becoming increasingly important in this discourse (Raus and Värri 2017, 107).

Although the inclusion of nature and animals has not been carried out equally in all scientific disciplines in the past (Kompatscher et al. 2017, 201–203), more recent disciplinary and interdisciplinary discourses show an approach to social dimensions of animals and actors in the more-than-human world.[2] In these, it is assumed that the actors speak for themselves and that purely objective studies of nature or animals are no longer regarded as up-to-date. Rather, power relationships and interactions between humans, animals, and nature are put into the context of interdependence and interaction that must be reflected upon (Gesing et al. 2019, 18–19). In this context, ethnographic analyses are particularly recommended, as they assume that natures and cultures are not only mutually dependent but also create each other (Kassam 2009, 47).

Ethnographic analyses of relations between humans, animals, and natures require access to scientific results and findings on different species, consideration of sociological analyses of cultures, and findings in the educational sciences.[3]

Current debates show a gap in the systematic investigation of the interdependent relationships between humans, animals, natures, and cultures and their complex interrelationships in (inter)disciplinary contexts (Gesing et al. 2019, 9; Jickling et al. 2018). The fields must therefore be adequately related in a holistic way in an inter- and trans-disciplinary form (Subramaniam 2019, 192–194; Kassam 2009, 17). Here, however, it is not a matter of dissolving the disciplines and developing a large uniform discipline, but rather of drawing essential elements from various sources in implementation in order to adequately describe interactions and relationships in HumansAnimalsNaturesCultures and to be able to map the interdependencies (Gesing et al. 2019, 10; Kassam 2009, 88–90).

The changes in the relationship between humans, natures, and animals are increasingly caused by the development of the digital world and must therefore be taken into account. Here it is apparent that the internet, natures, and animals are significantly influenced in their construction. A digitalized networking of animals, for example, by tracking whales, and the publication of this data in the "Internet of Animals" additionally influences the perception and construction of natures and animals. This development will change our understanding of how the internet has already transformed society (Pschera 2014, 97–98). The internet as such is initially alien to nature, as it is a global network of several calculating machines. However, this network provides opportunities to enter into virtual contact with nature and animals, although this contact is biophobic in the first instance. However, this does not mitigate the desire for virtual contact with nature, which appeals to the biophilic urge of humans (Pschera, 97–98). This assumption can be linked to the approach of the biophilia hypothesis, which describes a physical, cognitive, and emotional orientation toward living nature as an elementary meaning for human beings (Kellert 1997, 3). Following Merleau-Ponty's, Abram also assumes that humans do not only show an orientation toward the animate and inanimate environment but are rather closely connected to it; they are one with it (Abram 1996, 67). To document this connection and sensual impressions, he uses the language of writing, although he also finds himself reflecting on a barrier in the perception of nature (Abram, 71–72).

The predominant dichotomy between human/animal and nature/culture, which is discussed in various disciplines, attains an elementary significance especially in regard to Abram's assumption. Consequently, there is no 'either/or' answer (Brand 2014, 16; Alger and Alger 2003; Irvine 2004; Pschera 2014; Kaldewey 2011). The adoption of HumansAnimalsNaturesCultures forces, in addition to the transformative view of the actors themselves, the potential of individual disciplines and interdisciplinary dialogue on new and critical questions in a multispecies research. In order to promote this, a posthuman idea is necessary, which starts from a universal, essential, and biological reduction in the idea of humans, animals, and natures. Their cultural connections are linked in a creative way and through interdisciplinary cooperation (Hamilton and Taylor 2017, 181). In the spirit of Gesing et al. (2019, 10–12), the concept takes up heterogeneity and multiplicity in order to work out the intertwinements and limits of all actors in a holistic approach and to allow for new research strategies. In this context, it is particularly important to ensure the motivation and discourse skills of all participating actors relevant to breaking up existing structures and promoting innovative concepts. It must not be overlooked that a large distance between individual disciplines requires a complex organization in interdisciplinary cooperation. This applies not only to the cooperation between the individual disciplines but also to the consideration and implementation of a change in perspective in the view of nature and animals. For this reason, openness and the ability to force this change of perspective are indispensable. Only if an open disciplinary perspective is jointly pursued can hurdles concerning the change of perspective be identified and reasons for failure minimized (Bendix and Bizer 2011, 3–5). According to Kompatscher et al. (2017, 213), in the context of future multispecies research, research cooperation between the social sciences and natural sciences should be particularly consolidated in order to make a combination of relevant results from the disciplines useful for HumansAnimalsNaturesCultures. This is particularly relevant with regard to the holistic research in this area. For the inclusion of the more-than-human world as an actor in research projects, however, it is not sufficient to merely form interdisciplinary alliances—for example, between social and natural sciences—which work both jointly and separately according to realism and constructivism. Rather, each discipline has to specify the subject matter of humans, animals, and nature in such a way that new theoretical and empirical results are possible. In practice, this means that, with reference to system or action-theoretical theories, an interdisciplinary polycontextualization, which allows a multidimensional view, must take place (Kaldewey 2011, 279). To do this, academics should leave their own comfort zone, read theories from other disciplines, and work with them (Hamilton and Taylor 2017, 10). Interdisciplinarity is a crucial building block in future multispecies research and can only function through teamwork, interpersonal skills, and networks, although inconsistencies in research funding often make it difficult to work across discipline boundaries (Hamilton and Taylor 2017, 157; Bendix and Bizer 2011, 3–5). HumansAnimalsNaturesCultures, like the research area of human-animal studies, can be described as a metadisciplinary field (Marvin and McHugh 2014, 3), which is particularly important against the background of the acquisition of specialized knowledge (Daheim 1969, 365). Knowledge arises through social relationships and is constituted by individual perception, attribution of meaning, and types of knowledge (Daheim 1991, 29–30) Scientists often only perceive what is visible in the 'scientific community' and this visibility is frequently characterized by the interaction of politics, economy, and society (Kompatscher et al. 2017, 201–203). For the inclusion of humans, animals, and nature, this means that these can only be taken into account in the complex interrelationships if they are given attention and become visible within disciplines and across disciplines in research projects. What sounds simple in theory turns out to be challenging in methodological implementation, as the neutrality and objectivity of appropriate research methods is legitimized as a status quo. It is difficult to include the point of view of natures and animals without risking anthropomorphization.

In addition, an interpretation of the results always depends on the previous understanding and conceptualization of the research. According to Kompatscher et al. (2017, 206), this means that it is not uncommon for the ethical framework and assumptions under which research takes place to be ignored. Quantitative surveys, for example, have limitations in the analysis of complex private life forms because, for example, there are weaknesses in the construction of questionnaires, which lead to respondents misunderstanding questions or not filling them in at all. On the other hand, there is criticism concerning qualitative surveys and their lack of representativeness (Hamilton and Taylor 2017, 133). This does not mean, however, that research is fundamentally questioned. Rather, presumptions must be supported and questioned more strongly in order to secure evidence of HumansAnimalsNaturesCultures (Kompatscher et al. 2017, 201–203) and to reflect on the limits in the disciplinary and interdisciplinary analysis of animals and nature (Fudge 2017, 19). It is highly precarious, especially for the scientific landscape, if new and socially critical research areas are delegitimized and consequently excluded (Kompatscher et al. 2017, 204). Another important point in the discussion on HumansAnimalsNaturesCultures is the question of the scientific implementation of these new research methods, which are particularly relevant for multispecies research. The inclusion of animals and natures in the context of their relationships with human actors in research concepts of the various disciplines encourages in particular the further development of existing methods and the analysis of creative, complex challenges (Hamilton and Taylor 2017, 178). Hamilton and Taylor therefore call for an inclusive attitude[4] in order to not only look at animals anthropocentrically (Hamilton and Taylor, 201). The exclusion of individual actors from HumansAnimalsNaturesCultures in the various disciplines cannot be further adopted. Instead, the view is directed forward. It will be evaluated how multispecies research can succeed not only in the individual disciplines but also in interdisciplinary networks. This also involves using existing theories from the various disciplines and developing them creatively (Hamilton and Taylor, 178–179). The scientific habitus of the disciplinary 'scientific communities' will play a decisive role here if HumansAnimalsNaturesCultures are to be analyzed as an overall concept. For new forms of research, writing and teaching must be developed in an appreciative manner to achieve well-being for all (Hamilton and Taylor 2017, 180; O'Brien and Howard 2016, 118). The basis of Multispecies Ethnography is the idea of HumansAnimalsNaturesCultures as a creative and innovative model of the future society in a sustainable world. In Block's sense, this assumes a transformation of the concept of the environment to a concept of the world that resolves the constructivist and realistic conflict and promotes the interweaving of HumansAnimalsNaturesCultures into an inclusive "self-world *relationship*" (Block 2016, 17, emphasis added).

NOTES

1. Here, reference should be made to debates, which, for animal actors, denote the predominance of a culture, even though this culture is described, for example, in the case of monkeys, as persisting at one level (Tennie 2019). As another example, the culture of migration among moose is cited, which as behavioral strategies can promote the acquisition of resources, and condition culture (Middleton et al. 2013).

2. Ethnobiological and ethnozoological studies in particular provide an insight into the relationship between flora, fauna, animals, and indigenous and nonindigenous communities (Hunn 2011; Anderson 2011), which are often anthropocentrically oriented (Zarger 2011, 371).

3. This demand plays a decisive role, not least for current sustainability strategies and cultural cooperation both locally and globally. A close connection between humans, animals, natures, and cultures must be taken into account, since sustainable development processes, for example, cannot be explained by analyses of human behavior alone (Gesing et al. 2019, 9; Jickling et al. 2018).

4. The inclusive attitude describes in concrete terms elementary values, norms, and attitudes of researchers toward actors in the multiethnic world and the understanding of their agency to include and reflect on how subjective thinking and acting codetermines their own research projects.

Chapter 4

Multispecies Ethnography

The previous chapters have shown the importance of analyzing multispecies relationships in the context of HumansAnimalsNaturesCultures and the potential that arises here in interdisciplinary cooperation. The present chapter focuses on the question of the methodological implementation of precisely these analyses of relationships and relations between humans, natures, and animals. Multispecies Ethnography, which is described synonymously as interspecies ethnography (Madden 2014, 279–281), has become established for the analysis and research of these relationships. The English terms 'multispecies' or 'interspecies'[1] are used in the various disciplines to clarify that humans and other species are closely related to each other. While interspecies ethnography has been used to analyze relationships between different species, Multispecies Ethnography follows a more inclusive understanding. In addition to interspecies relationships, it incorporates multidimensional orientations of the collective and provides a complex analysis of interdependencies within and outside species boundaries. This analysis is planned and carried out systematically and purposefully in the research design so that the (positive) outcome is a dissolution of rigid boundaries between humans, animals, and other life forms (Fenske 2016, 291; Madden 2014, 279–281).[2]

The development of Multispecies Ethnography is based on research by scientists from various disciplines who have made it clear that an "essentialism of nature" (Ogden et al. 2013, 11) exists. This led to a focus on the way in which the natural environment, animals, plants, and culture are interdependent (Gesing et al. 2019; Buschka et al. 2012). The impetus in the development of Multispecies Ethnography can be traced back to the increase and interest in (empirical) research based on the more recent research directions on human-animal-nature interactions. This boost has positively led to the reflection of relevant research methods in recent years, especially in the English-speaking

49

world. In this context, Multispecies Ethnography has emerged as a methodology with potential, especially for the study of interactions between humans and animals. While it is only carried out sporadically in German-speaking countries (Fenske 2016, 302), in English-speaking countries, it is already being implemented in human-animal studies (Kirksey and Helmreich 2010, 545–547; Moore and Kosut 2014, 526; Hamilton and Taylor 2013, 176–178).

Multispecies Ethnography is generally recruited for research work that recognizes the connectedness and inseparability of humans and other forms of life, such as plants or animals, and thus expands classical ethnography (Locke and Münster 2015; Spannring et al. 2015, 17–19). The fact that "the fund of sociological statements on the possibility of interspecific social relationships (. . .) is extremely modest" (Teutsch 1975, 24) allows the assumption that it is precisely the analysis of these interspecific interactions between humans, natures, and animals that offer a decisive research opportunity in the future, for example, to combine the findings of ethology with those of sociology, as Alverdes (1925) already attempted to do. Multispecies Ethnography makes looking at relationships between humans and plants and animals or bacteria and viruses in an interdisciplinary way possible (Ogden et al. 2013, 10), as it recognizes that there is interdependence between human life, agriculture, and technologies (Locke and Münster 2015).

> In other words, Multispecies Ethnography is a project that seeks to understand the world as materially real, partially knowable, multicultured and multinatured, magical, and emergent through the contingent relations of multiple beings and entities. Accordingly, the nonhuman world of multispecies encounters has its own logic and rules of engagement that exist within the larger articulations of the human world, encompassing the flow of nutrients and matter, the liveliness of animals, plants, bacteria, and other beings. (Ogden et al. 2013, 6)

Multispecies Ethnography documents cultures, perspectives, and practices in a multispecies world by depicting the immersion of life in a shifting collection of acting beings (Hammersley 2006, 4). The view and perspective on natures and animals can sometimes be difficult and frustrating because it reveals boundaries. These can be overcome, at least in part, by methodologically, theoretically, and politically promoting the inclusion of nature and animals in scientific research processes and recognizing their agency. This requires a transformation of research that incorporates empathy and novel methodology (Hamilton and Taylor 2017, 194–196) and breaks down the category 'human' with its symbols, discourses, and institutional segments (Pedersen 2011c, 67).

The considerations for implementing Multispecies Ethnography go back to the debates on dichotomies in human-animal and human-nature interaction described in chapter 2, as well as to the assumption that it no longer seems tenable to erase other species from one's methods. This leads both scientists and the 'scientific communities' to question their own self-image and whether it is justifiable not to include particular individuals in research, because standardized procedures do not capture essential characteristics, such as emotions or language in animals. This critical self-reflection of one's own understanding, as well as established scientific methods and theories, allows innovative research designs, which successfully include nature and animals. This creates the opportunity to develop methods that allow complex multi-species research. Within this methodology, animals and plants are taken into account by accepting the fact that they possess knowledge and agency. By including other species and expanding in the sense of an open and exploratory research design, species-related one-sided methods and theories can change in an inclusive way (Hamilton and Taylor 2017, 182–183). Hamilton and Taylor call this a "species-turn" in all disciplines (Hamilton and Taylor 2017, 79), since interlocking processes of doing, experiencing, and living together in a world with many others are explained (Hamilton and Taylor, 124). This finding is supported by political and feminist theories, which address the interfaces of global discourses on nature conservancy, animal protection, sustainability, and the effects of the use of nature and analyze them in the context of lifestyles (Gesing et al. 2019, 11). The analysis of these interfaces is made possible by means of (ethnographic) studies by selecting several research locations and the simultaneous encounter of several species within the contact zones (Haraway 2008, 8) with, for example, animals, plants, fungi, or bacteria (Hamilton and Taylor 2017, 24). Through Multispecies Ethnography with bees, Fenske illustrates, for example, that, in addition to the bees themselves, listening to the beekeepers is an essential part of the collection of research data in order to map the complexity of multispecies interactions (Fenske 2016, 303). The same applies to communication with plants, fungi, or bacteria. In the best case, experts should be consulted whose experience and knowledge can be incorporated into multispecies research. However, the barriers between species mean that despite relevant progress in multispecies research, many unknowns remain (Fenske 2016, 291).

4.1 HISTORY OF ETHNOGRAPHY

Ethnography basically describes a research methodology, which analyzes groups of people, societies, and cultures. Classical ethnographic research projects can be found in various disciplines and contexts, although they have their origins primarily in the cultural and social sciences. Literary studies in particular practiced ethnography of texts early on and over a long period of time, thereby creating a stage for other disciplines (Mauss 2013, 19). In

recent years, a wide range of research results and manuals have emerged
(e.g., Heidenmann 2011; Smartt Gullion 2016; Breidenstein et al. 2013;
Underberg and Zorn 2013; Thomas 2019), which is why the following two
sections 4.1. and 4.2 provide only a brief overview of the history of 'classical'
ethnography. The two sections do not aim to provide a far-reaching and broad
reception of all facets of ethnographic research (for this see, for example,
Thomas 2019; Breidenstein 2006; Breidenstein et al. 2013). They serve as
a basis for the derivation of essential core elements for further development
toward a Multispecies Ethnography. 'Classical' ethnography finds its roots in
British social anthropology, American cultural anthropology, and the qualitative sociology of the Chicago school (O'Reilly 2009, 3; Madden 2014, 279).
Therefore, in the Anglo-Saxon world, the term is used synonymously with
the terms 'cultural anthropology,' 'social anthropology,' and 'ethnology'
(Honer 2000, 196). Especially the ethnographic records of foreign cultures
can be traced back to antiquity. They originated in colonialism and developed
to observe and describe indigenous peoples. In the further course of time,
ethnographic research expanded to include one's own society, by conducting
studies of groups that were culturally neighboring. Ethnography thus enabled
a mixture in the analysis of foreign cultures and simultaneous analysis of
the familiar (Honer 2000, 196). In addition to Franz Boas, who spent longer
research stays with indigenous peoples in the 1890s, one of his students,
Margaret Mead, also conducted ethnographies to identify the connections
between culture and personality. Initially, the focus was on the analysis of
human nature, to analyze how society functions, education is practiced, and
other people are treated. In this way, routines and rituals were recorded and
analyzed in the context of objects and artifacts (Hamilton and Taylor 2017,
30–31; Budde 2015, 15–16). By going into the familiar environment of the
participants and collecting a variety of interactions with them, researchers
were able to understand societies, institutions, and cultures (Madden 2017,
17). Through Bronislaw Malinowski and Radcliff Brown, the participating
observation in particular became more widespread, as the previously conducted analysis of second-hand data gave way to field research. This was
characterized by the fact that ethnographic field research was conducted 'on
site' over a period of more than a year. The two researchers went into the
field, lived with the researched people over a longer period of time; learned
and practiced their language, rituals, and cultures; and collected data. This
direct cultural immersion was aimed at exploring the connections between
objects, people, systems, and organizational structures. To this end, the
effects of the research on those being researched, as well as the emotions
evoked by it, were also reflected upon in order to ensure the depiction of a
great totality (Mathews and Kaltenbach 2011, 150–152; Eriksen 2001, 14–16;
Hamilton and Taylor 2017, 30–31).

The ethnographic methodology spread and, as the Chicago School progressed, led to the analyses of social life, more specifically social interactions, participation, and memberships in organizations. Consequently, social groups were increasingly studied ethnographically and commonalities and differences were elaborated (Hamilton and Taylor 2017, 32–34). The 1920s also saw the creation of further important influences for ethnographic fieldwork and the establishment of further impulses based on Herbert Blumer's (2013) symbolic interactionism and Erving Goffman's (1974) work. Thus, participant observation was transferred to modern societies and the importance of direct contact with people in everyday situations was emphasized, as well as Goffman's focus on the context-related roles of people (Mathews and Kaltenbach 2011, 152).[3] The inclusion of audio-visual recordings in later works on ethnography does not, however, make it clear, in Goffman's sense, that reference is made exclusively to this database. Rather, a pluralist position pursues the use of different materials "in order to gain alternative and complementary approaches to the subject and possibilities for comparison" (Willems 2000, 44). Budde nevertheless believes that participant observation, along with a presence in the field, is the core of ethnographic research (Budde 2015, 8). "Neither laboratory simulations, biographical self-testimonies, nor surveys or statistical procedures can bring the implicit routines and the practical knowledge embedded in them to analysis—here, too, the specific significance of participant observation as a central method of ethnography is founded" (Budde, 13). Ethnography developed further into interpretative research (Mathews and Kaltenbach 2011, 38), in which the social reality of others was mapped through the analysis of one's own experiences in the world of these others. Here, language serves as a basis for symbolic representation. This also applies, for example, when there is no direct correspondence between an experienced world and the world in a text, but there is a correspondence between the observed and the observer (van Maanen 1988, ix; 8). Language serves as a guarantor for noting and writing by eliciting what words or symbols mean, symbolize, or signify in a social interaction. Consequently, language constitutes an essential translational function in ethnographic research (van Maanen 1988, ix; 8; Hamilton and Taylor 2017, 40; Kuhn and Neumann 2015, 29).

In the 1990s, a more pragmatic analysis finally came into focus, which Budde describes as a praxeological turn (Budde 2015, 8). This gave rise to different research that now analyzed multiple objects, animals, and their interactions with humans. This trend, which became known as the sociology of technology and science, was particularly influenced by Bruno Latour (1995) and Michel Callon (1987) (Hamilton and Taylor 2017, 41–42). At the same time, this development led to a decline in micro-sociological research due to increasing doubts. The skepticism about ethnographic research resulted from the described expansion of the method by collecting highly diverse data from artifacts, spaces, animals, or objects (Budde 2015, 14–16). At the same time, this necessitated a reflection on the concept of action, so that action was henceforth described in a praxeological sense "as a momentous movement of body, language and/or artefacts in social space" (Budde, 14). This development allowed for new insights and questions, although their theoretical construct was not conclusively discussed (Kuhn and Neumann 2015, 26). While ethnography has experienced an increased application in the US-American area—as has already been shown—it is currently still in a developmental process in Germany (Thomas 2019, 14; Lüders 2000, 384–386). Although ethnographic research projects are increasingly practiced (Pole and Morrison 2003; Breidenstein et al. 2013; Atkinson et al. 2001; Delamont 2012; Thomas 2019), it is currently not conclusively clarified whether ethnography is a "research style that is methodologically plural" (Bohnsack 1997, 3), a research strategy, and a methodology (Lüders 2000; Breidenstein et al. 2013). The only thing there seems to be an agreement on is that an application of the entire toolbox of methods can be pursued in the field (Thomas 2019, 2). In recent years, there has also been a growing interest among academics in ethnographic research in posthumanism. In the age of the Anthropocene, posthumanism describes a constructive response to contradictory social conditions, situations, and consequences of the contemporary world. This results in cross-disciplinary interlockings that analyze the perspectives, activities, and actions of humans, animals, and natures as actors of the (more-than-) human world in social contexts in a multiperspective way in (Hamilton and Taylor 2017, 41–42). For this, the basis assumes a system of "intertwined disciplines" (Mathews and Kaltenbach 2011, 149–150), in which interface research occurs, which uses the capabilities for dense "descriptions and (. . .) two-way translation at system boundaries" (Schönhuth 2018, 95). The development of Multispecies Ethnography is situated within posthumanism (Hamilton and Taylor 2017, 44). However, the current research style and status of the methodology is not conclusively established and discussed in the context of the role of the "research species" (Hamilton and Taylor 2017, 44).

4.2 CHARACTERISTICS AND METHODS OF ETHNOGRAPHIC RESEARCH

Currently, there is a large variety of ethnographic research methods that "methodologically refer to the position of the manifesto in a more or less unambiguous way, and at the same time proceed methodologically very differently" (Budde and Meier 2015, 3). In ethnographic practice, for example, there are participant observations, ethnographic interviews, and participant research techniques that are developed and adapted in the context of the research design (Pink 2015, 7). Thus, there is not one standard way that is generally practiced, but many different and intersecting variants.

Ethnographic research generally observes social phenomena in a precise and complete manner (Mauss 2013, 47). In the classic form, this involves "writing about people" (Madden 2017, 16), which is defined ethnically, culturally, and socially. This results in an exploration and understanding of social lifeworlds that allow for transformative processes (Madden 2014, 279–281; Pink 2015, 7–9; Hamilton and Taylor 2017, 148). Ethnography thus resembles a process of creating and representing knowledge (about society, culture, and individuals) that is interwoven with ethnographers' own experiences. Ethnography does not claim to be objective, truthful, or realistic but serves to document experienced versions of reality. These are to be presented as loyally and realistically as possible to fit the context, so that negotiations and intersubjectivities that generate knowledge are included (Pink 2015). Ethnography is consequently a creative methodology that presupposes a sympathetic attitude toward other people and involves both openness to new experiences and ways of thinking and a practicing network-building (Hamilton and Taylor 2017, 133; Dellwing and Prus 2012, 12).

Ethnography does not, first of all, fundamentally aim to develop systematic theories, but rather pursues the mapping of the diversity of dimensions of the research field where previously only the surface was scratched (Mauss 2013, 21). This implies that ethnographic research per se cannot be controlled. This can be illustrated by the example of a laboratory situation. These are usually highly standardized in order to achieve the best scientific results. Ethnographic research, on the other hand, is fundamentally characterized by an open and explorative approach in real settings (Madden 2017, 17). In comparison to 'artificial' laboratory research, the aim in an open setting is to combine inductive and deductive perspectives in an interactive way so that a "bottom up" and "top down" is carried out in the sense of grounded theory (Madden 2017, 18; Pink 2015, 7–9). This enables construction and deconstruction through an intensive look at what is observed. For this, "Doxatic self-evident truths and claims to validity of one's own culture are inhibited [and] moral evaluations and prejudices are suspended" (Madden 2017, 21–22). This means that significant and insignificant details are openly presented and made visible, so that a view of one's own and foreign cultures opens up. In principle, then, it is about observing human actors in their daily lives (and in their cultures), listening to them and asking questions. The resulting reports and stories are documented, the role of theory is recognized by researchers and thus all actors are included as a subobject/part of the research (O'Reilly 2005, 3).

This results in the relativization of one's own culture from the perspective of the foreigner. This opening is not self-evident because, for example, volatile judgments are not automatically openly visible (Madden 2017, 21–22).

In order to draw a holistic picture of ethnographic research, research must take place in a team, with researchers setting out together and practicing an interdisciplinary approach to data collection. This ensures the classification of observations and interpretations in their complexity and from different perspectives (Mauss 2013, 14).

Mauss illustrates this with the example of a ceremony: Although it takes place actively and directly before one's own eyes, it cannot be perceived and seen in all its manifestations. "There is nothing that is self-evident" (Mauss, 18). Only documentation, archiving, and interpretation allow for complex analysis. This is decisively shaped by the multi-professional role of the ethnographer and the exchange in the interdisciplinary team (Mauss, 18).

Objective science with subjective representation does not represent a contradiction for Mauss, since objectivity and subjectivity cannot be separated (Mauss, 15). This view is also taken up by Aikenhead and Michell in the context of indigenous cultures. Objectified 'universal' research results float in a culture-free space, as it is assumed that human and worldly elements do not interfere with each other. This leads to the assumption that realities do not change (Aikenhead and Michell 2011, 29). In the authors' view, however, this perception is unfavorably chosen, since one cannot assume a scientific method that depicts universal laws without subjective elements. Rather, scientific methods are dynamic and tentative (Aikenhead and Michell, 42–44). Hamilton and Taylor underline this by emphasizing that emotions and thoughts are masked by human filters in the research process, regardless of the procedure (Hamilton and Taylor 2017, 187). This conditions that in all scientific disciplines there is a balance between subjectivity and objectivity. Despite this, high standards are necessary to map and reflect the different practices and variants in ethnographic research in their specificities as well as the limits of the methodology (Hamilton and Taylor 2017, 187; Mauss 2013, 16). Relevant practices and variants are described by Mauss as "geographic and demographic statistics, museography and lexography, ethnobotany and ethnozoology as well as the archiving, inventorying, collecting, mapping and cataloguing of all social facts of all things and their uses, of actors, animals (body) techniques, games, rites, practices, institutions, arts" (Mauss 2013, 16). Mauss' openness to the diversity of methods, data, and evaluation procedures used is viewed critically by Budde and Maier, as the two authors are skeptical about the simultaneous use of different practices. In this context, they point to the existing consensus among researchers, since ethnographic research materials range from photographs and documents to biographical interviews and standardized questionnaires as ethnographic data. However, the inconsistent regulation leads to open questions of method triangulation, the implementation of data triangulation, as well as the implementation in the analysis of the collected data (Budde and Meier 2015, 4–6). The indeterminacy of the various practices in particular requires a focus on normativity, so that the focus is shifted to reflective knowledge (e.g., in pedagogical practice) (Budde 2015, 9–10). In the sense of Bourdieu (2005), one's own standpoint outside the research event must therefore always be reflected upon in order to counteract an inseparability of subjectivity and ethnography. This inseparability constitutes the highest potential and at the same time the greatest weakness, as it cannot be methodically controlled (Budde 2015, 12–13). Reflection is thus of essential importance, in that one's own self is always also constructed in the construction (Kuhn and Neumann 2015, 32; Bollig and Neumann 2011).

> Doing ethnography is probably the most demanding way of performing qualitative research. It takes a lot of time, the capacity to interact with a variety of people, the management of an ambiguous role, and at times real physical discomfort (. . . .) But it also offers a whole range of very interesting possibilities and challenges. It is, in some ways, the royal way of doing qualitative research. (ten Have 2004, 7)

Only the success and interlocking of all core areas with the interaction of all participants allows for 'being ethnographic' (Madden 2014, 281), so that observations are carried out extremely objectively and thoroughly (Mauss 2013, 50). This requires a complete physical and psychological presence in the field in order to participate, observe, write, and analyze (Hamilon and Taylor 2017, 27; 45–46). Despite all subjectivity, Hamilton and Taylor, in contrast to Budde, assume that "being objective" means that many variants of data are collected in research diaries/protocols (Hamilon and Taylor 2017). In this context, a detailed thoroughness is important that does not neglect any detail in ethnography and thus carries out an open and deeper analysis. In order to practice this thoroughness, observations are sometimes hardly sufficient, so that further documents, such as cultural texts or statistics, are consulted (Hamilon and Taylor 2017, 27; 45–46; Mauss 2013, 50). In the next step, this intensity allows for in-depth observation and analysis (Hamilon and Taylor 2017, 27; 45–46). The connecting 'being native' is embedded in the conceptualization of ethnographies and follows the risk of a lower analytical distance (Budde 2015, 11).

In the concrete implementation of the methodology, such as in participant observation (Madden 2014, 282; Mauss 2013, 23), researchers enter the field with all their senses and record rituals and motives on-site through structural and targeted observations (Madden 2014, 282; Madden 2017, 19; Schulz 2015, 44). They approach, explore, and analyze the so-called foreign (Budde and Meier 2015, 3). "All the senses belong to this experience. Not only seeing and hearing, but also physical and emotional feeling" (Spittler 2001, 19). Here, eyes and ears are systematically used for observation in such a way that researchers are able to adapt to the situation and do the same activities as the observed (Madden 2014, 282; Madden 2017, 19). The body of the observer and his or her associated body language hence play a significant part in the interaction and in conditioning it (Madden 2014, 282; Mauss 2013, 23). The observer can thus be described as an "organic recording device" that embodies subjective empiricism (Madden 2014, 282; Madden 2017, 19).[4] This subjectivity and personality of researchers must be adequately taken into account in the research design and with regard to the research question (Kiepe 2004, 24). Schulz states that

> sensual, self-referential, bodily-sensual or subject-constitutive data such as feelings, impressions and experiences that can be considered close to the body or the bodily (. . .)—in comparison to what researchers see and hear—are exposed to far less public reflection in these representations. (Schulz 2015, 45)

This view is also shared by Abram, who uses the example of interaction between humans and nature to justify that all senses must be used for perception. Their description in the form of written language, though, could not be presented conclusively in all details (Abram 1996, 129–131). However, this should not mean that avoiding this problem of representation leads to them not being reflected upon as well (Schulz 2015, 45).

In addition to the role and implementation by researchers, the ethical justifiability of the research, the specific research design and appropriate documentation of what is observed are just as relevant core variables of ethnographic research as the final ethnographic data analysis (also Thomas 2019). The analysis of the data is carried out with the help of all senses, so that physical and tactile experiences take a back seat. Through this and the inclusion of reflexive processes, meaningful conclusions can be drawn (Budde 2015, 11; Madden 2017, 19; Daly 1984, 394–395). In the course of the evaluation process, a deep understanding of the facts and inner connections plays a decisive role in establishing links. For this, the interplay of a differentiated theoretical basis is just as important as an intuitive approach, which per se is already scientifically questioned.

Dense descriptions, objective hermeneutics, or grounded theory are often used for the evaluation system (Thomas 2019, 26; 115). The reference back to theories and research question(s) allows for an illumination of blind spots by drawing on existing knowledge without leaving out openness and the recognition of non-knowledge.

In the end, ethnography provides stories, statistics, and a realm of certainty about the researched field (Mauss 2013, 47–49), which ultimately offers classification in social phenomena through the collected and analyzed observations, interactions, and textual analyses (Hamilton and Taylor 2017, 27–28).

According to Hamilton and Taylor (2017, 29), the theoretical concepts underlying new ethnographic analyses are posthumanism, postcolonialism, and queer studies. However, these underlying theories for ethnographic research primarily relate to humans and have hardly been discussed in the context of multispecies research. Following Marcel Mauss, it can be assumed that the study of animals will take on a high status in future ethnographic research, as areas around ethnozoology and ethnobotany will find consideration in ethnographic analyses (Mauss 2013, 29–30). Relationships to animals (nutrition, care, breeding, medical care, means of payment, aesthetics, theory, and roles) can be analyzed ethnographically, as can wild, medicinal, field, and cultivated plants (Mauss, 29–30). Individuality and commonality are not contradictory. Rather, everything is connected, bound, and networked with everything, so that humans and animals in particular are described as belonging together in a mythical promise of kinship (Mauss, 44). Ethnography thus provides the innovation and creativity with which posthumanism enters. Animals, plants, and natures as complex entities hence play a role in all disciplines in which they enter research contexts as actors (Hamilton and Taylor 2017, 69–71). Traditional ethnography is methodologically expanded and researchers test new forms of methods and finally implement them in their disciplines as Multispecies Ethnography.

4.3 THEORIES OF AN ETHNOGRAPHIC MULTISPECIES RESEARCH

The present chapter serves as a kind of open concept in questioning and deriving underlying theories that seem relevant to multispecies research in general and Multispecies Ethnography in particular. Thus, the chosen theories are not to be seen as rigid and fixed, but as a selection of helpful and appropriate theoretical concepts. They are intended to serve as puzzle pieces in the further analysis of the research field and methodology and to be expanded in the future by (inter-)disciplinary perspectives and theories. Theoretical puzzle pieces will be reinserted or already faded pieces will be replaced by new ones. This calls for interdisciplinary cooperation to identify further suitable theories for holistic multispecies research in general and Multispecies Ethnography, in particular. Currently discussed theoretical approaches underlying Multispecies Ethnography engage with various related philosophical and social-science endeavors. These approaches attempt to rethink the construct around nature and society. They include, for example, object-oriented ontologies, hybrid geographies, post-structuralist political ecologies, posthumanism, and the exploration of science and technology for alternative epistemologies. These concepts can already be understood as basic foundations for future multispecies research (see for more detail: Ogden et al. 2013, 6; Fudge 2017, 6).

Furthermore, symbolic interactionism is particularly suitable for Multispecies Ethnography in its basic framework as a foundation of interaction relations. In addition, post-actor network theory and indigenous theories are considered relevant, as these two theories recognize networks of HumansAnimalsNaturesCultures.

Symbolic Interactionism

Goffman's interaction theory (1974) is used for multispecies research because it has already been adapted for human-animal relationships (Irvine 2004). 'Interaction theory' first describes a social order framed by social situations. Here, perspectives of reality arise in the shaping of individual interactions. Social interactions and encounters are characterized by physical presence and require individuals to enter the sphere of influence of other individuals in a physical environment. Goffman distinguishes between centered and non-centered interactions: Centered encounters characterize a concrete, conscious interaction in which the actors actively concur and maintain cognitive and visual attention. Non-centered encounters, on the other hand, assume the presence of two individuals in the form of interpersonal communication within a space (Goffman 1974, 67; Sander 2012). Interactions here are characterized by a 'confrontation' of actors in which each actor operates on the basis of how this situation is classified (Blumer 1997, 4). According to Rock, this conditions the close connection between symbolic interactionism and ethnography (Rock 2002, 29).

For the ethnographic analysis of human-animal-nature relationships, the interaction ethology developed by Goffman (1974, 10) can be consulted. This approach, originally related to the human-human relationship, allows a transfer to human-animal-nature relationships against the background of current social developments. In HumansAnimalsNaturesCultures, close relationships are assumed that are characterized by interactions and thus allow for an extension of the 'classical' interaction partners. Interactions in HumansAnimalsNaturesCultures are accompanied by an assumption of roles that requires making visible the meaning of the interaction and the symbolically attributed value of objects (Abels 2007, 50–52).

However, this also implies that misunderstandings or a lack of role adoption can lead to shifting interpretations and thus distort the meaning of forms of communication. Goffman's theory is used as a relevant basis for classical ethnography, since an analysis of interaction processes requires proximity to the researched and a naturalistic and authentic approach (Goffman 1996, 263; Willems 2000, 43). In establishing a "deep familiarity" (Goffman 1996, 267), it is necessary to venture directly into the lifeworld of the researched. For multispecies research, this means that humans conducting research follow the animals or plants into the respective field, and eat, work, and live with them. This co-becoming enables a direct contact of the rituals and routines of animals, humans, and natural processes as well as the mapping of intentional and non-intentional interrelations. The inclusion of nature and animals in research processes also enriches current debates and allows us to answer the question of what it ultimately means to act socially (with them) (Irvine 2004, 177). Research on this has already been described by Alger and Alger (2003) using the example of a cat shelter or by Irvine (2004) for the general human-animal relationship.

Alger and Alger use the example of an ethnographic analysis of cats to illustrate that they would carry out norms, roles, and sanctions and implement them within their "cat culture" (Alger and Alger 2003, 48). "We connect, know, think, secularize, and tell stories with and through other stories, worlds, forms of knowledge, thoughts, desires" (Alger and Alger, 134). This happens in all diversity and in a category-breaking speciation and interconnectedness by making all relationships in time and space visible (Alger and Alger, 134). Although curiosity initially leads researchers a little far from the path, it is precisely in these remote places that the stories lie (Alger and Alger, 176). The authors conclude that animals, for example, are able to apply symbolic interactionism, whereas this is not discussed in depth for microbes or fungi.

Nevertheless, it is virulent to want to reconstruct the object of natural and animal research on the basis of subjective experiences, as these approaches in particular seem limited and too anthropomorphic at first glance. Still, it is helpful to use Multispecies Ethnography to reconstruct interactions and social relations within HumansAnimalsNaturesCultures and to see the world through the eyes of different species. This is especially necessary in the context of a changing planet. All rules must be broken, and previous knowledge questioned and transferred to other species. Only in this way can both an explanation of HumansAnimalsNaturesCultures be undertaken and their interactions with each other be analyzed as cooperating and competing entities in inter- and intra-specific relationships (Haraway 2018, 91–93).[5] For this, an interdisciplinary consensus is essential that detaches from old models and directs the perspective toward new and transformative angles to allow for the development of new models (Haraway, 95–97). This is relevant for future sustainability research, as it is precisely here that there is an increased focus on uncomfortable questions and that cross-species co-becoming and co-doing must be practiced (Haraway, 141). An example of a cross-species question in the sense of co-doing and co-becoming would be: "What happens without the bee?" This question can be analyzed and answered under ethnographic research and from different (inter-)disciplinary perspectives in the context of social interactionism. Biotic and abiotic (out)effects of biocultural, biotechnical, biopolitical, historically situated actors are compared and combined here (Haraway, 137).

Actor-Network Theory

In addition to symbolic interactionism, actor-network theory (ANT) is considered to be of particular importance, as it allows the discomforts of the world to be made visible and their construction to be questioned (Latour 2008). ANT assumes that actors function as actants and enter into a network. Following Luhmann (1984), Kaldewey describes Latour's actants as equivalent to a subject/object assignment, which is, however, harmonized by an ontological notion (Kaldewey 2011, 284). Humans, natures, and animals join together in networks as actants and interact dialogically (Callon 1987, 151–153; Bell 2012, 225). Despite the heterogeneous actors, a stable network can be recognized, which is characterized by convergence and mutual behavioral coordination. At the same time, the interactions between the species are characterized by irreversibility, which can cause changes in the individual interactions and weaken the network (Bell, 225). This results in an interaction and recognition of intertwined pathways between humans, natures, and animals, which have already been discussed (Peuker 2011).

Post-ANT currently no longer exclusively assumes a so-called network and actors as actants but describes actors as forming a collective (Latour 2008, 1; Peuker 2011, 154–156). Here, both no unity as a network and no separation are made, because it is precisely these that give rise to conflicts in the first place. This implies that an exclusive inclusion of HumansAnimalsNaturesCultures is assumed by not making a separation. Latour's ANT thus establishes the basis of the network and the demarcation of science education in the first step and shows the complexity in the relationship between humans and the more-than-human world in the second step. The link to the post-ANT makes it possible for HumansAnimalsNaturesCultures, through a research-oriented approach, to make connections visible, without pre- or post-discriminations of actors in the network. This makes it possible to identify and illustrate highly complex connections (Kropp 2015, 206–208). At the same time, ANT (Latour 2008) allows hybrids of facts and beliefs to emerge (Bell 2012, 225).

Although ANT softens the boundaries between humans, nature, and animals and fundamentally allows for an analysis of HumansAnimalsNaturesCultures, the construction of these relationships and the individual actors must be analyzed in greater depth in the future. This results from the criticism of the empirical verifiability of this theory (Kurth et al. 2016, 26–27; Peuker 2011, 154–156).

Indigenous Theories

In order to undertake a study of HumansAnimalsNaturesCultures, Multispecies Ethnography is relevant to the analysis of all actors and the collective, as the symbolic nature of interactions is taken into account. Multispecies Ethnography is thus used for research that recognizes the interconnectedness and inseparability of humans and other life forms such as plants or animals, hence extending classical ethnography (Ogden et al. 2013, 10). It recognizes that there is an interdependence between human life, agriculture, and technology (Locke and Münster 2015) that is significant for a sustainable lifestyle.

It is a methodology that seeks to understand human subjectivity and utilize it for education and our engagement with nature. This in itself highlights the need for the inclusion of indigenous knowledge, especially to bring the agency of nature and animals more into focus. A transformative process is initiated to connect the theoretical pillars for Multispecies Ethnography in an inclusion of Western theories and the methods of indigenous cultures (Aikenhead and Michell 2011, 114). This means that the previous exclusion is replaced by an inclusive mindfulness in the analysis of the research, as it is assumed that humans and nature cannot be considered and analyzed in a detached way (O'Brien 2016, 126; Abram 1996, 52).

This realization of the inclusion of indigenous knowledge and theories goes back to the finding that indigenous knowledge is a relevant instrument in transformative research processes, even though this knowledge has been largely ignored in the scientific discussion of methods in recent decades (Kincheloe and Steinberg 2008, 135–136). The reason for this is partly to be found in the character of Western sciences, which, similar to the omission of indigenous knowledge, also excluded nature and animals in parts in disciplinary terms (Aikenhead and Michell 2017, 7). Nevertheless, indigenous groups provide alternative knowledge and perspectives based on their own locally developed practices of resource use, which is helpful in the context of multispecies research (Berkes et al. 2000, 1251–1253). Following the development of indigenous pedagogical concepts, initial transformative processes in research methodology can be stimulated and used for multispecies research.

For this purpose, in order to break down existing stigmas, it is advisable to start not from an indigenous worldview, but from scientifically compatible worldviews (Berkes et al., 27). These include the following:

1. Promoting the reorientation of research;
2. Focusing on the ways in which knowledge and methods are produced and legitimized;
3. Inclusion of indigenous knowledge and theories in the development of a multispecies ethnography and the elaboration of relevant theories (Kincheloe and Steinberg 2008, 140–142);
4. New levels of epistemological interest.

It is therefore logical that the complexity and multilocality of Multispecies Ethnography should take into account the inclusion of indigenous theoretical concepts, although this will require further research and the inclusion of indigenous cultures in the development of Multispecies Ethnography (Kincheloe and Steinberg, 138–139). Even though these elementary areas cannot be duly covered within the framework of this work, exemplary reference will be made to a research work that illustrates the significance of nature in indigenous peoples.[6]

In 2014, Magallanes-Blanco used participant videos to analyze the significance of nature for indigenous peoples in five different countries. Based on a letter from Chief Seattle, it becomes clear that for indigenous cultures, the earth does not belong to humans but humans belong to the earth. They are inseparably connected to it and thus influence the networks attached to it (Heinämäki 2009, 5). A similar definition is given by the World People's Conference on Climate Change, which understands "Mother Earth" as a unique, indivisible, and self-regulating community of interconnected beings that sustains and reproduces all beings (WPCCC 2010). Whitehouse et al. (2014, 9) also agree with this. The living environment has a right to integrity, which is illustrated by the example of the Maasai: The river, for example, has the right to have trees along its riverbeds as well as to contain sand in the bottom that purifies the water (Magallanes-Blanco 2014, 204). This understanding of indigenous peoples points to a dialogical relationship that is characterized by cultural favors and rituals with nature. In this context, it does not have a negative connotation if human attributions are used for this purpose and behavioral patterns are assigned (Hersch-Martínez et al. 2004, 27–29). "The Maasai consider that a balance between the natural elements means sustainability and happiness for every element of nature" (Magallanes-Blanco 2014, 207). Indigenous cultures can be understood as essential actors in the development of future Multispecies Ethnography (see section 4.5 for more details) (Magallanes-Blanco 2014, 202).

4.4 BASIC IDEAS, OPPORTUNITIES, AND
LIMITATIONS OF MULTISPECIES ETHNOGRAPHY

In an extension of classical ethnography, Multispecies Ethnography assumes an inclusive attitude toward plants, animals, and other life forms of the more-than-human world as well as an openness to interdisciplinary research projects. This inclusive attitude is a great asset for the (inter-)disciplinary methods in research projects on HumansAnimalsNaturesCultures. Fenske describes, for example, collaborations that test ethnological and ethological approaches in human-animal relations (Fenske 2016).

An interdisciplinary cooperation between the sociological and veterinary disciplines should be mentioned here as an example. Here, both disciplines approached each other through the field of human-animal relationships and initially pushed the development of an educational offer for animal-assisted services in equal parts. This offer was implemented in an interdisciplinary team and in the implementation of nature-based and animal-assisted learning for different professional groups and with reference back to sustainable education (University of Giessen 2018). In the further course, this real-life cooperation developed into a deeper and essential research project in the analysis of a culture of care for the field of experimental animal science. The culture of care is characterized by communication and appreciation of humans and animals but also by the attitude and professionalism of the professionals toward humans and animals. The establishment of the culture of care aimed at by the project outlines the path to be taken in order to meet the required legal, but also ethical demands (ICAR3R 2019). The described collaboration between sociology and veterinary medicine hence pursues the use of collaborative possibilities that have arisen, to change perspectives within the disciplines and to open up to multispecies.

As already demonstrated in chapter 2, the exemplary disciplines pursue fundamentally different research foci and methodological designs. With regard to the establishment of multispecies research, however, it is evident that both disciplines jointly see a higher added value of an interface analysis for transformative concepts in HumansAnimalsNaturesCultures and explicitly utilize this added value, here using the example of the culture of care. This added value also needs to be expanded for scientific research in general, since the natural and agricultural sciences are only in rudimentary contact with cultural and social-science disciplines in the context of HumansAnimalsNaturesCultures. This results from different methodological approaches and the theories and concepts used, which are partly contradictory. For this reason, cooperation between different disciplines is always a challenge that requires openness and the crossing of boundaries in professional action (Fenske 2016, 2017). Openness is understood as a key for joint research in the context of interspecies relations based on known and new methods. This can be further promoted firstly through (inter-)disciplinary collaborations and secondly through the inclusion of indigenous knowledge; it nevertheless poses challenges for interdisciplinary collaboration. This results from the fact that, for example, indigenous knowledge is often far removed from the natural sciences and its inclusion means a high degree of openness and willingness to experiment. As a result, instead of conducting research side by side, close cooperation between disciplines is carried out and relevant findings from one's own discipline are made accessible to the other discipline and supplemented by indigenous knowledge. Consequently, research is located in the individual disciplines and then—through a connection with other disciplinary fields—related to each other (Fenske 2016, 304–305).

Multispecies Ethnography enables—despite existing boundaries—different disciplines to tie in with the existing methodology and to complement it with their own methods as well as to include indigenous knowledge. In this respect, interdisciplinary cooperation resembles a dance between subfields and disciplines, which is hardly imaginable at present, and which is not described in more detail in the research field of multispecies research. Interdisciplinarity, intersubjectivity, and empathy are essential core elements in the application of multispecies analysis and require the inclusion of relational capacity and an empathy toward data (from other disciplines) (Fenske 2016, 291; Hamilton and Taylor 2017, 29; Schulz 2015, 49). This presupposes a fundamental recognition of agency on the part of all actors, described in German-language contexts as 'Handlungsmacht' or 'Handlungsträgerschaft' (Kurth et al. 2016).[7] The recognition of this agency in the research context specifically includes empathy for different species. This allows us to talk about what it is like to be (like) the other. However, it does not answer the question "what it is to be 'with' the other" (Despret 2004, 128). "The act of moving and listening, rather than participating, talking, asking questions and observing is prioritised" (Despret, 124). One's own experience is included in the sense of sensory ethnography and analyzed in a text-centered way (Schulz 2015, 49). Foster is an example of this. He carried out an analysis from the perspective of a badger by living in a replica badger's burrow and eating earthworms. In doing so, he pursued the goal of broadening his own perspective and thereby ensuring that it is possible to adopt a different perspective—namely that of another species (Foster 2016). This approach is already described as an innovative form of research in the analysis of human-animal relationships (Hamilton and Taylor 2017, 119–120), although this does not allow the automatic conclusion that the taste of the worm is also comparable for a badger.[8]

An interspecific perspective described in human-animal studies thus attempts to see everything "through the eyes of an animal." Madden states this using the example of the analysis of cats. It is elementary for researchers to think like a cat (Madden 2014, 279–281). For this, a transgression of boundaries—in the sense of one's own boundary—is necessary, since species do not speak the same language among themselves and Western researchers in particular have lost the ability to understand other species (Abram 1996, 145; Daly and Caputi 1987, 51; Kincheloe and Steinberg 2008). Additionally, it must be argued here that humans cannot even put themselves 1:1 into the shoes of another human being (Fenske 2016, 290). Ethnographic methods in the analysis of human-animal interactions thus reach their limits, for example, in direct human-oriented communication with animals. This results from the fact that they are designed humanistically and the 'thoughts'[9] of the animals cannot be easily captured. Furthermore, we cannot easily learn and practice the language of other species (Fenske 2016, 291).

Consequently, cultural rules and so-called pigeonholing must be reflected just as much as communicative peculiarities. Nevertheless, the opportunity is taken for animals and nature to perceive their interests and to put them on paper (Hamilton and Taylor 2017, 58–59). This requires particular sensitivity when references to animal races or gender are made, as this can lead to stereotypes and social norms (Hamilton and Taylor, 113).[10] In this context, Budde notes that biographical questions cannot in principle be dealt with using ethnography, as ethnography focuses on actions and processes rather than biographies, which makes it difficult to measure competences with the help of ethnography (Budde 2015, 12–13). In contrast, Fudge explicitly demands that biographical questions should also be asked in regard to other living creatures and natural processes. The reconstruction of these biographies allows an approach to animal and natural biographies, which have not been sufficiently considered so far (Fudge 2017, 8–10). Hence, Multispecies Ethnography offers the possibility to construct the agency of animals and nature in such a way that what is visible is also made visible as such (Fudge, 19). In doing so, however, animals and nature must be taken into account not only conceptually but also methodologically (Hamilton and Taylor 2017, 12).

The empirical basis of Multispecies Ethnography involves observing the relevance of different types of knowledge in the respective field of study. This includes in particular the view of the living creature, such as animals or plants. Fenske illustrates this with the example of analyses of human-animal relations. She understands this as animal research, which, in turn, describes a form of knowledge research. The analysis of these relationships refers to the observation of the relevance of different types of knowledge in the respective field of study, but—from the perspective of the cultural and social sciences, which are rather less trained in the view of the living animal—also to the reception of knowledge from natural science research (Fenske 2016, 303).

Kompatscher et al. (2017, 201) see a challenge in the implementation of Multispecies Ethnography concerning the integration of animals' or even plants' agency into research. They ask in what form and manner the experiences of animals can be disclosed without omitting distancing and differentiation processes. These questions and those of how empathy is created toward plants and animals will come into focus in the future in order to meet the limits and challenges of methodology, to bring in the animal's and/or plant's point of view and to establish neutrality and objectivity within this complex structure. The fragility of objectivity is exemplified by Helena Pedersen (2011b) in a study with chickens, where an ethology student reflected on her objectivity during the research and came into conflict with the scientific culture. The objective facts—here exemplified by experiments with trained and subsequently tested chickens—became holey when she reflected on them subjectively. The researcher showed this through emerging doubts about reliability and controllability in the execution of the experiment. Although the chickens involved inevitably remained in the test situation[11], they could very well influence the experiment through their individual actions. Thus, it was possible for the chickens, as acting individuals, to disturb, delay, complicate, or change the experimental arrangement. Although the observing researcher perceived this influence and ultimately found the qualitative data more trustworthy than the quantitative data collected, only the test scores expected by the "scientific community" were published (Kompatscher et al. 2017, 205).

From this example, Kompatscher et al. argue that data "are hardly ever objective and clean, but multidimensional, complex and messy, and methods less rigid and waterproof than often assumed" (Kompatscher et al. 2017, 206). Interpretations of results depend on the prior understanding and conceptualization of the research (Hilbert 2016). Accordingly, it is hardly possible to conduct research outside the human point of view and to depict in detail what exactly a being senses. Nevertheless, this does not exempt research from including other beings and creating an approach. This applies both to research in general and to human-nature or human-animal relationships in particular (Kompatscher et al. 2017, 208). Markus Wild (2013) proposes anthropomorphism as a heuristic tool to guide Multispecies Ethnography (Kompatscher et al. 2017, 208). This approach is also affirmed by Despret, who assumes that humanization mediates new identities. The experience of humanization enables the contestation of new paths to a "new humanity" and consequently new identities (Despret 2004, 130). Gebhard also recognizes that animals and the (anthropomorphic) ensoulment of nature (subjectification) allow a reference back to inner and unconscious parts of human soul life.[12] This does not mean that 'real' natural phenomena are faded out, but rather that the tension between natural phenomena would be interpreted animistically anthropomorphically. "Knowledge of nature (i.e. objectification) and symbolic ensoulment (i.e. subjectification) are not mutually exclusive" (Gebhard 2013, 70). Through this, Multispecies Ethnography can take several paths. This can be illustrated with the example of a lobster by analyzing ecological conditions of the population as well as describing its life up to its capture in a literary anthropomorphic way. Objectification and subjectification are represented by complementary approaches to reality, which need neither exclude nor contradict each other. Both together generate a true understanding by giving accurate descriptions and individual meaning (Gebhard 2013, 70).

For this purpose, non-anthropomorphic and lifeworld experiences as well as emotional and mental abilities of animals cannot be excluded; rather, it is precisely these that must be analyzed (Jones 2019, 298). In this context, Serpell (1985) states that emotions have a significant influence on how distanced something is perceived. Hence, the emotional value of animals often decreases when they are used for economic purposes. This accentuates the fact that predator and prey are equally anthropomorphic (Gebhard 2013, 70) and that "emotional (. . .) anthropomorphic relationships to nature are culturally undesirable and are dismantled when the economic exploitation of nature is in the foreground" (Gebhard 2013, 72).[13] Consequently, it is necessary to question practices in the human-animal-nature relationship (in research) and to make the agency of the more-than-human world visible. This is done by taking into account nonverbal forms of communication and bringing in empathy and sensory experiences through a Multispecies Ethnography (Despret 2004, 213). It must be taken into account that human abilities to carry out ethnography represent a limit for animals or plants. However, these limits should not tempt us to exclude nature and animals as a collective with the power to act in research projects, but to create methodological and theoretical flexibility in how and in what form research is conducted with other species (Hamilton and Taylor 2017, 45). Multispecies Ethnography must always critically consider and reflect in the research process, which power processes, dominance, and exploitation exist, as well as which of these aspects are relevant within (one's own) research (Hamilton and Taylor, 110).

4.5 (INDIGENOUS) CHARACTERISTICS OF A MULTISPECIES ETHNOGRAPHY

The application of Multispecies Ethnography presupposes a holistic approach and the acceptance of an agency of nature and animals or actors of the more-than-human world. This includes that the world and the way it is shaped is 'multispeciestical' (Hamilton and Taylor 2017, 45). Including nature and animals enables us to direct and understand both the animality of animals and human life in the context of referring back to the aliveness of trees, rocks, stones, and

apparent 'objects' (Ogden et al. 2013, 17; Cajete 2000, 86). Indigenous societies make particular use of 'storytelling' for this purpose. This allows connections to be made visible, although indigenous cultures in particular are very
careful in their selection of people with whom knowledge is shared (Cajete
2000, 87; Houde 2007, 1–3).[14] Cajete refers here, for example, to a story of
his grandmother who taught him respect for the world, the use of plants and
their health effects (Cajete 2000, 87). Observations and generated knowledge
are hence validated and linked through indigenous social life (Houde 2007,
1–3). In addition, indigenous ecological knowledge[15] often shows a strong
connection to the particular place where indigenous communities are located.
This deeper knowledge of places is essentially taught and learned through
nature. Here, especially factual and specific observations are given a superior
role, which are not about analyzing facts about animals, their behavior, and
their habitat, but about deducing connections between species or historical
trends. It is thus also about mapping the dynamics of systems (Houde 2007,
1–3). This describes a close connection that is primarily established through
social symbols, rituals, art, future-oriented indigenous knowledge, and vigors,
in order to connect with animals, plants, water, mountains, the sun, the moon,
and the stars (Cajete 2000, 95–97). Animals and plants are always included so
that an explicit role attribution takes place, which is supported for indigenous
relationships with the world by the biophilia hypothesis, even though: "Native
Science is a people's science, a people's ecology" (Cajete, 99–100).

Native Science is characterized by observations that are a core element
of indigenous cultures and that are reflected in knowledge and ways of acting. For Multispecies Ethnography, this means in its methodological form
that within observations, plants and animals are understood as mentors and
the existing relationships are valued by researchers, by them becoming one
with the species and the world (Cajete 2000, 104; Aikenhead and Michell
2011, 79–81).[16] This means more precisely that, similar to classical ethnography, in Multispecies Ethnography, research is also conducted with all the
senses—by being at and in the place. This ensures an authentic view of the
research object and does not separate emotional, moral, economic, social,
political, and cultural aspects (Aikenhead and Michell 2011, 79). In addition
to seeing, tasting, hearing, touching, healing, and intuition, established tracking systems have already been used for multispecies research (Aikenhead
and Michell, 102). This means, conversely, that complexity is hardly being
hidden. Rather, multispecies research plays out contingencies, although it is
precisely these that make research so particularly difficult because so many
interrelationships have to be taken into account and yet remain unknown
(Linkous Brown 2006, 50).[17]

Emily Yates-Doerr (2019, 227) describes this in reference to her (multispecies) ethnographic analyses on the topic of meat: Multispecies Ethnography is

intended as a stimulus to analyze the possibilities in which relationships arise. In doing so, the design of humanness and human kind as well as their relation to other living beings must be resolved. Multispecies Ethnography consequently does not pursue a categorization of objects or exclusions, but rather focuses on their emergence and dissolution. Following on from this, Dalke and Wels describe that the ethnographic analysis of HumansAnimalsNaturesCultures in particular can be animal- and nature-friendly research, as it explicitly recognizes and analyzes the connections between body and body, mind and mind, as well as matter and matter (Dalke and Wels 2016, 192). For this, Pedersen raises the question that all disciplines must ask themselves: Do we only want to learn about animals and plants, or also with them? (Pedersen 2011b, 24).

Multispecies Ethnography, following indigenous theory, hence basically assumes that there is an ordered and complex web of living entities in which each subarea has its purpose and meaning as well as cause and effect. This intricate structure mapped (Pierotti 2015, 81). For the implementation of Multispecies Ethnography in the sense of Buber (1999) and Snauwaert (2009, 98–100), empathy, inclusion, and the I-You relationship must be taken into account as criteria that establish direct contact between subjects through intersubjectivity and build consensus through transsubjectivity:

1. Empathy in Multispecies Ethnography describes an empathizing with actors in the human and more-than-human worlds. Here, one's own concreteness is to be excluded to such an extent that differences move into the background. This enables a subjectivity that allows a connection with the other actors.
2. Inclusion describes a meeting of individuals with individual perspectives, so that differences are maintained and a simultaneous participation in reality takes place. This requires a direct understanding of the other within oneself by encountering the other in the concrete uniqueness as a subject.
3. The I-You relationship describes an interdependence between the I and the You. The You is the present part that stands opposite the mysterious part of the other. The You thereby forms the subjectivized view of the other through intersubjectivity and transsubjectivity (Snauwaert, 98–100).

The connection of the criteria requires a work of translation that allows the ego as such to recede into the background and permits indirect and direct interactions. These allow visually, sensorially, and digitally a natural and free behavior as well as a wealth of data, for which the processes taking place are fully mapped in their complexity and multiperspective views are taken (Mathews and Kaltenbach 2011, 155; Hamilton and Taylor 2017, 148; Breidenstein et al.

2013, 187). Here, disruptive factors, the preparation, and follow-up of individual interactions as well as lifestyles and habits are included. This is intended to contribute to an independent interpretation and memory performance that enables a deduction from the results (Mathews and Kaltenbach 2011, 155), which, as an independent version, promotes something new (Breidenstein et al. 2013, 187).

For this, as already indicated, the application of all senses—which are not separated but closely connected—is necessary. Sardello and Sanders distinguish these into world senses, which include smelling, tasting, seeing, and feeling warmth, and into the higher senses, which include hearing, speech, thinking, and individuality (Sardello and Sanders 1999, 234–240). The environment is perceived through smell, which means that researchers take in the world through their bodies. This is significantly characterized by intimacy. Smelling and its manifestations cannot be simply and automatically coded linguistically. Rather, smelling enables the basis of a moral evaluation of the situation, even though it is not an evaluation in the strict sense but merely offers the possibility of classifying something morally. Tasting describes a culturally reshaped sense, since this is how the world is evaluated. It allows the transition zone between body and world to be established and is more active than smelling. This results from the fact that smelling is permanent, while tasting is selective. Sight describes a feeling sense that allows intellect and shows how the world is perceived. Seeing does not refer exclusively to looking with the eyes, but integrates feelings intellectually. For instance, it becomes apparent that perceiving colors, in contrast to perceiving shapes, is an emotional form of seeing. Autumn, for example, is perceived differently from summer because seeing enables different perceptions and classifies them. Seeing is also closely connected to all other senses, since tasting is described through seeing, and the balance is regulated through seeing (Sardello and Sanders, 237–238). The sensation of warmth is described as the soul of the senses within the framework of the world senses, since the sensation of warmth or temperature balances the world of feelings from the outside and feeds back to one's own person. It is tied to our interest in the world and the world with us (Sardello and Sanders, 39).

The authors describe the higher senses as hearing, speech, sense of thought, and individuality. Hearing allows us to perceive the inner qualities of the outer world as well as to depict worldly experiences of the spiritual nature or those of the human being through the body. Basically, what is perceived as language is what wants to be heard. A selection is made through evaluation, feeling, and classification. Speaking and hearing are mutually dependent and also show close connections to the sense of thinking. Thinking of other persons and processes requires practice in order to really understand what the other person means, says, and feels. In the context of Multispecies

Ethnography, it is necessary that the act of thinking is enjoyed and carried out in the spirit of childlike openness and experimentation (Sardello and Sanders, 243–245). The last higher sense describes individuality, which is about perceiving, accepting, and valuing the other person as an individual. This is described as a spiritual act, as the acceptance of otherness is like stepping out of one's comfort zone and thus represents a challenge for the research process in the form of a spiritual level. This illustrates the importance of a fusion of indigenous and western scientific approaches, which must be trained in early education in order to be adequately usable (Sardello and Sanders, 244–246). This includes the reflection on one's own worldview, culture, and spirit (Absolon 2011, 52). This approach can be used as a transformative model for Multispecies Ethnography if Multispecies Ethnography is to establish itself in the long term. As a consequence, it is necessary that a consciously critical approach is chosen within the framework of Multispecies Ethnography in order to perceive the holistic nature of dependencies and interdependencies (Absolon, 52). This means more specifically for the research process that holistic methods, theories, and practice are combined and included in the research process in order to elaborate and reflect actions and visions on realities. This also includes the classification of one's own worldview, a critical placing of one's self and the prevailing processes, and the subsequent placement in the context of world and self (Absolon, 165–166). This aspect is not exclusive to Multispecies Ethnography. However, the factor is weighted higher due to the required holistic view.

4.6 TYPES OF MULTISPECIES ETHNOGRAPHY

There are different types of ethnography that have been named and applied in different works and publications. The types of Multispecies Ethnography can be applied from living in the research environment through active-participant or participant observations, to video or photographic observations, or to diaries in the form of autoethnographies. They thus correspond in principle to 'classical' ethnography, whose subareas are preserved in their core elements and adapted and further developed for Multispecies Ethnography. This refers especially to the methodological integration of animals, plants, and natures in the sense of an inclusive methodology in (inter-)disciplinary research networks. The development of Multispecies Ethnography is therefore based on the types and concepts of classical and, here, especially sensory ethnography. The result is that "ocular- and verbal-centered field research methods, observation and interview, are complemented by other, usually neglected, sensory approaches" (Kubes 2018, 50). In the following, different approaches in multispecies research will be outlined. Although these are described separately, they are to be understood as combinable and interdependent for multispecies research.

(Classical) Autoethnography

Autoethnography represents a particular subfield of ethnography and is of particular importance for Multispecies Ethnography as it represents a method and a process as well as an outcome. A multispecies autoethnography combines personal with sociocultural experiences and allows them to be systematically processed (Adams et al 2019, 2–5; Ellis 2004, 1999, 676).

Autoethnography is characterized by the personal involvement of researchers, which is evident in the fact that their personal experiences are analytically processed. In addition to field experiences, "one's own actions, thoughts, experiences and perceptions become the object of observation and analysis" (Boll 2019, 33). Kuhn (1967) found that the vocabulary of researchers is closely linked to the realities found in the construction of universal narratives (Adams et al. 2019, 2). In the 1970s and 1980s, however, this finding led to a debate on the representativeness of ethnographic research—the so-called 'crisis of representation' (Berg and Fuchs 1993)—which had the consequence that a separation of researchers, their research results, and the researched involved was viewed critically. This eventually led to a rethinking of the forms and purpose of sociocultural research and description (Ellis and Bochner 2000; Adams et al. 2019, 2), from which autoethnography in its current form emerged (Ellis and Bochner 2000).

Although some scholars still assume that research has to be neutral and objective, research in recent years has shown that different worldviews, ways of speaking and writing, and forms of evaluation and beliefs have an influence on the construction and conclusions of researchers (Kompatscher et al. 2017, 201–203; Breuer et al. 2019, 4–6; Bonz 2014, 37–39; Denzin et al. 2017; Adams et al. 2019, 3).

Multispecies autoethnography describes an ethnography of one's own experience in which researchers are both subject and object and "in whose narratives emotional experiences and personal, concrete-everyday and inner-worldly details are described" (Schulz 2015, 50). In order to practice systematic autoethnographic research, one's own reflective capacity plays a particularly important role (Hamilton and Taylor 2017, 69–71). Self-observation and self-reflection must be carried out in depth and precisely so that interdependencies between researchers and researched are recognized (Adams et al. 2015, 2). Boll takes this a step further by identifying a level of "observation of *observation* itself, as participant and research practice, and complementary to this, the observation of the generation of *observability* as an effect of the observed and observing practices" (Boll 2019, 35, emphasis added). Autoethnography is therefore not, in the sense of Geertz (1990), an "egocentric navel-gazing" (Schulz 2015, 51), but provides the deconstruction of biographical self-representation and self-construction through a precisely dense writing. For the most part, stories are told in first person and interpreted through the lens of personal culture. This is done by including the personal experiences of researchers; questioning their cultural beliefs, practices, and experiences; and discovering and acknowledging the close relationship with 'others' (Adams et al. 2015, 1–2; 2019, 4).

Autoethnographies have been carried out especially in the field of cross-border research, but have not yet been explicitly extended to include animals and plants. What is needed is an extension of observations from a triadic view[18] that also takes the surrounding environment into account (Adams et al. 2015, 71). This leads to a broadening of perspective that allows for the observation of narratives of animals and plants and thus looks at the world not on but with animals and plants. This resembles an addition and illustrates that kinship is rethought by dissolving species boundaries; in the sense of Donna Haraway's "Make kin, not babies" thesis[19] (Haraway 2018, 140–141, 178). Here, as a participating observer, it is possible to analyze how "others perceive reality, act, desire—are subject" (Bonz 2014, 37). This applies to both humans and actors in the more-than-human world and allows for a holistic and new view of relationships between humans, animals, and natures.

These findings are documented in the form of diary entries, documents, letters, photos, or drawings and are co-reflected with regard to one's own subjectivity as a methodological tool (Bonz 2014; Adams et al. 2019, 4). In addition, there is the possibility of drawing on other research findings such as interviews, observation protocols, or artifacts (Adams et al. 2019, 4–5). Autoethnographies are characterized on the basis of analyses. For example, Adams et al. (2019, 6–8) elaborate the following types, which are also relevant and transferable to the context of multispecies autoethnography:

1. Carried out on the basis of researching the "foreign," indigenous ethnographies are based on one's own experiences and cultural narratives (Denzin et al. 2008).
2. Reflective ethnographies document the change of researchers in the course of the research process (Adams et al. 2019, 6).
3. "Layered accounts" focus on the process character within research processes, in that data collection and analysis proceed simultaneously and questions and comparisons are used as sources (Charmaz 1983, 110).
4. Interactive interviews and collaborative autoethnographies describe the sharing of experiences through joint conversations and over a longer period of time, where interaction is understood as a collaborative research process (Adams et al. 2019, 7).

5. Co-constructed narratives focus on relational experiences and ambivalences within and outside relationships, and practice a shared analysis (Adams et al., 7).
6. Personal narratives focus on the narration of researchers, but without resorting to deeper analyses or the accompaniment of scientific literature. This form has been heavily criticized (Adams et al., 7).
7. Analytical autoethnographies describe a symbiosis of traditional qualitative social research and elements of autoethnography in order to "gain new theoretical insights, refine existing theories and transfer theoretical concepts from one context or case to other contexts and phenomena" (Adams et al., 7).

Due to the orientation of autoethnographic research, it is particularly important that ethical concerns are taken into account. For research subjects who are in close relationship with the researchers, anonymization is not always possible in an appropriate way. This can be problematic for researchers themselves and must be taken into account ethically in the research design (Adams et al. 2019, 9).

Emotions are of particular importance in multispecies autoethnographic analysis (Adams et al. 2015, 5). The inclusion of emotions from the perspective of researchers makes revealing unnoticed, hidden insights possible.

The extension of this approach is described as Living Fieldwork. This refers to a research method "that seeks to combine autoethnographic approaches with 'classical' research designs" (Kubes 2014, 112). For multispecies autoethnography, this means a combination of participant observation with sensory ethnography, which allows for particularly difficult phenomena to be researched. For this, the participant role and the researcher role are not separated, but completely immersed in the world of meaning, and a 'feeling and doing' is practiced in equal measure. In this way, researchers themselves become research objects. Only by leaving the field is the separation between field and science re-established (Kubes 2018, 285–287).

Multispecies Ethnography through Media Ethnography

Media ethnography describes a methodological "approach in qualitative social research, the aim of which is to describe and document and interpret the social and cultural practices of the production of media as well as the use and reception of media of all kinds in an ethnographic way" (Bergmann 2008, 328). Through the medialization of society, visual methods allow for the development of innovative forms of representation. In the past, for example, these were used especially for the analysis of historical-social construction of animals and were carried out through visual images, videos, and artifacts (Bergmann, 330–332).

In this context, the pictorial documentation in photographs allows for the original representation of social reality through historical evidence and cultural social practices that are represented iconographically. In comparison, videography shows a primary recording of interactions that can be watched repeatedly (Thomas 2019, 88).

By taking pictures or videos of animals, plants, or nature, the actors in the photo or video become the focus of research.[20] This allows for the analysis of everyday interactions. This can be, for example, going for a walk (with a dog), a ride on a horse, or a visit to the zoo. Pictures and videos can always have the ability to provoke or shock (Thomas, 92). In the analysis of photography or videography, both the subject itself and its relationship between similar and dissimilar actors—independent of language—are discussed and analyzed (Thomas, 93–94). Images and videos are categorized as objective and subjective in equal measure, since they are recorded in reality and interpreted by the viewer in excerpts (Thomas, 97–98). Although a processing of the images can stir up both positive and negative emotions, the inclusion of positive and negative emotions is necessary. This ensures the consideration of neutrality and rationality (Thomas, 100).

An analysis of photographs in an interdisciplinary team and with the help of Multispecies Ethnography hence allows researchers, students, and practitioners as well as the photographed subjects to participate in the research. The inclusion of all actors takes place through their active involvement in the research context by making the concrete relationships visible. Through this, feelings and impressions (excitement, calm) are shared as well as thoughts and conclusions in a multispecies world. However, it must be taken into account in the analysis that photographs do not allow for auditory observations and can thus evoke other emotions than, for example, video recordings (Thomas, 100).

Videography or cyber ethnography focuses on an ethnographic analysis that does not take place in a face-to-face situation in a real setting, but overcomes temporal and spatial boundaries (Madden 2014, 284; Thomas 2019, 89). Here, the internet, which is both a field of information and a cultural field, serves as a basis for documentation (Markham and Stavrova 2016, 299–301). Hence, websites, downloadable text, or film files, as well as social platforms, can be integrated into the research process (Thomas 2019, 89). Madden (2014, 284) describes the juxtaposition of a real versus a virtual sociality in such a way that the virtual world represents a real world, which, however, must be thought of as more digital than analogue, although so-called parallel virtualities exist in the minds of people in all societies. For example, sexual partners or the weekly shopping become a real social digital interaction (Boellstorff 2008). All the feelings that take place in real life also take place in the virtual world. Virtual sociality is therefore not a fake, but real. Sociality is thus conceived as a series of communicative networks, machines, users, and animals that transform themselves within the networks. This raises the question of how nature and animals are methodically included (Hamilton and Taylor 2017, 53–54).

Cyber ethnography is characterized by networked research that maps the connections and interdependencies of virtual humans, animals, and natures and includes the consideration of digital development (Müller 2011, 59).

The relevance of a visual and digital multispecies observation lies in the conclusion that all human concepts can also be used for animals, plants, and all living creatures. In this context, it is irrelevant that the concepts are human as such, since, for example, precisely the behaviors of humans and animals are similar (Bekoff 2004, 495). First of all, the human perspective is maintained in that the observations are always described beginning from the perspective of the self. Hence, they become 'like me' and not 'human-like' (Milton 2005, 261). In addition to one's own human perspective, the perspective of the animal or other actors in the more-than-human world is always taken into account. In order to implement this, it is significant that the personal perspective on the research field is repeatedly questioned and reflected upon in the research process. However, despite many ideas, the fact that we do not have 1:1 the same experiences as another living being remains true (Nagel 1974, 438–439). Nevertheless, senses, corporeality, participation, and learning in community represent foundations of this ethnographic form (Kompatscher et al. 2017, 213). Observations enable evaluation of behavior, even though observations are difficult to practice without interpretation. This is because visual and auditory stimuli are processed at all times, and are compared with one's own learning experiences and thoughts. For this reason, they are particularly susceptible to subjectivity (Hasemann 1964; Grümer 1974, 11–13). This means that the methodology requires a high degree of reflexivity on the part of the researchers in order to adequately take into account the sources of error in their own research and the uncertainty of their own results (Hamilton and Taylor 2017, 133).

However, their analysis requires a different approach to research due to extended aspects. Madden assumes that the behavior of the observer and learning through shared experiences play a more significant role than a pure face-to-face interaction. This results from the fact that the world is seen through the eyes of the observer (Madden 2014, 284).

The visual methodology bears the danger that 'other' objects are also marked as such. For the more-than-human world, this could mean that it is perceived exclusively as an artifact instead of an actor (Hamilton and Taylor 2017, 101).

Multispecies Ethnography of the Senses

The inclusion of all senses is of high importance in ethnographic research in general and in Multispecies Ethnography in particular. The difficulty lies in capturing the perception and inclusion of the body in language and at the same time to reflect on the (supposed) subjectivity (Arantes and Rieger 2014, 13).

This debate—also known as *sensory ethnography* in the Anglo-American world—discusses a rethinking of ethnography in relation to the senses. It states a series of conceptual and practical steps in the ethnography of the senses that make it necessary to rethink already-established views and to experience new participatory and collaborative research techniques in the context of sensory perception, categories, meanings, and values as well as ways of knowing and practicing (Pink 2015, 7–9). This requires an intensified engagement with one's own corporeality, bodiliness, and sensuality as well as the analysis of these perceptions in the everyday life and in research processes. This approach is often closely linked to autoethnographic approaches and the goal of revealing discrepancies between "bodily enactments of feelings and bodily states of sensation" (Arantes and Rieger 2014, 15). It is therefore a multisensory participation of the researchers, who carry out a "walking with, eating with, sensing with" (Pink 2015, 7). This allows for a broadening of perspectives on the role of sensory perception in multispecies ethnographic research projects. Furthermore, it highlights a reference to the interconnections in HumansAnimalsNaturesCultures mentioned by Donna Haraway (2018, 67). Pink therefore calls for the inclusion of all the researcher's senses to be practiced self-consciously and reflexively throughout the research process in order to map these interconnections. The reflection and documentation of sensory perception should also be applied to the planning, review, fieldwork, analysis, and presentation processes of a project (Pink 2015, 7–9).

Moore and Kosut illustrate this with an example from their ethnographic research with bees. Bees, for example, can only be perceived through a limited range of human senses. What we smell, taste, hear, and feel, in addition to what we think about bees, is filtered and diluted by humanity and thus characterized in methodology by anthropomorphization (Moore and Kosut 2014, 525 ff). Nevertheless, smelling, tasting, feeling, touching, hearing, and seeing are central to multispecies research and allow the world of honey bees to be experienced and understood to some extent (Fenske 2016, Moore and Kosut 2014). This can be supported by interdisciplinary interfaces to implement sensory, artistic, and visual methods of ethnography. In the process, disciplinary boundaries and their relevance disappear (e.g., Hamilton and Taylor 2017, Kompatscher et al. 2017).

Jen Wrye then states, following Latour, that there are no unique human qualities. Rather, inanimate objects possess the qualities attributed to them by humans—the same is true of animals and plants (Wrye 2009, 1051). In Pink's sense, this entails the inclusion of the senses within field research while at the same time reflecting on one's own construction and independence of the discipline.

This approach is also found in the subject-centered method of Living Fieldwork, which has already been explained for autoethnographies. Nevertheless, the Living Fieldwork shows an access to "emotion, body and body disciplining techniques, emotion change and emotion acquisition" (Kubes 2014, 112), which are a cornerstone in sensory introspection. These guarantee the systematic analysis of sensory and emotional experiences and its ability to explain social theories and practices for HumansAnimalsNaturesCultures.

Art-Based Methods

Another methodology to implement Multispecies Ethnography is described by Hamilton and Taylor in the form of art-based methods. This can be implemented in the specific form of a theater, for example, and is hence particularly suitable for nonscientific audiences (Hamilton and Taylor 2017, 132).

This type of Multispecies Ethnography can be assigned to performance ethnography and describes an aesthetic theatrical methodology in which participant and observer roles are combined to artistically represent cultures. This creates a (de-)centered presence in which the focus is not on understanding the content, but rather a re- and de-construction of perception is undertaken and processed for the audience (Schulz 2015, 51; Geimer 2011).

However, art-based methods have not yet been widely received, although Hamilton and Taylor assume that the inclusion of nonscientific actors would allow for deeper and new insights into the complex relationship between humans and the more-than-human world (Hamilton and Taylor 2017, 132).

They illustrate this with the example of a 'cultural animal workshop', which was implemented with the help of a poem method. The audience used the opportunity to work on a topic, communicate with each other, and name problems in the context of multispecies (Hamilton and Taylor 2017, 140–142). This does not presuppose any knowledge or special skills on the part of the participants, but explicitly demands the artistic elaboration and reflection of social structures.

This can be illustrated in more detail by the development of a script—based on field notes—for an ethnodrama. The field notes were first collected and analyzed and then edited into a script (Hamilton and Taylor 2017, 136). The collaboration of different artifacts and interviews facilitated in the data collection process allowed, in the first step, the fundamental aim of ethno-dramatic methods, namely to break down boundaries between academics, practitioners, and society in order to practice transdisciplinary performance with participants (Hamilton and Taylor 2017, 137). This is more deeply differentiated, transformatively included, and analyzed for multispecies research.

Hamilton and Taylor state that the possibilities of artistic approaches to relationships between humans and the more-than-human world would go beyond rational and cognitive ones and hence allow for new forms of understanding these relationships. Although these are currently still under-represented, the two authors see a great opportunity in them (Hamilton and Taylor 2017, 147).

NOTES

1. Multispecies Ethnography is contrary to speciesism, which describes an unequal treatment of individuals on the basis of their belonging to other biological categories. Speciesism is still widespread also in the scientific disciplines (Noske 2008, 77–79). Multispecies Ethnography is one way of methodically countering this.

2. Multispecies Ethnography is not the same as multisited ethnography, in which the object of study is mobile and multiply located. These multiple localizations are initially perceived as separate worlds, but in the further course of the research process, they are linked to each other. This, however, refers exclusively to human actors, including a combination of different geographical and social fields (Ekström 2006, 502; Halbmayer 2010).

3. The first critical voices about the ethnographic approach emerged during this period. Criticism was voiced that it was not clearly recognizable whether it was actually a scientific method. The criticism resulted from the sociality of the researchers in the field who represented the method (Hamilton and Taylor 2017, 35).

4. Pyyhtinen (2016, 79) states with Straus (1963, 351) that both the becoming of the subject and the events in the world unfold in sensory experience. The now of feeling belongs neither to objectivity nor to subjectivity alone, but necessarily to both together. In feeling, both the self and the world unfold simultaneously—for the feeling subject; the feeling being experiences itself and the world, itself in the world, and itself with the world.

5. However, this causes problems to arise in the established and familiar routines of the scientific community. Contesting new research paths can lead to disagreements with reviewers, publishers, colleagues, and other disciplines (Haraway 2018, 95–97)

6. For the indigenous characteristics of Multispecies Ethnography, see section 4.5.

7. With regard to indigenous knowledge, agency can also be characterized as the belief that the earth is in itself a living being with rights whose protection is guaranteed by indigenous peoples (Doolittle 2010, 286).

8. Pink describes, following Simmel (Simmel 1997 [1907]), that his sociology of the senses provides a basis for ethnography. In Simmel's sense, Multispecies Ethnography can be understood as the attribution of meaning, mutual sensory perception, and influence for the social life of humans and the more-than-human world, in their coexistence, cooperation, and opposition. Similar to the other sociological classics, his understanding refers only to human actors. Nevertheless, for nature and animals, it can be assumed that senses take on a special role in communication, since hearing, smelling, tasting, and seeing play an essential role in the perception of the environment.

9. Here it must be stated that a thought describes something that is translated into linguistic form in order to be perceived as such. This makes clear the limits of the perception of these thoughts by actors in the more-than-human world, which is why it is often assumed that animals, for example, have no thoughts (Perler and Wild 2005).

10. For Fudge, it remains unanswered whether the stories of animals put on paper represent another kind of human history or a humanism in disguise (Fudge 2017, 5).

11. The research design consisted of 33 chickens from a laying battery and the student. The aim of the project was to check whether cage rearing has not only negative physical effects but also negative psychological effects.

12. The rational view of humans, nature, and animals seems to overshadow animistic thinking and thus determines the relationship to the world (Gebhard 2013: 69).

13. Gebhard (2013, 72) poses the question here, especially for educational processes, to what extent the abolition of anthropomorphism has a function for the education of children and young people, who are almost trained out of this ability in adolescence.

14. The North American Mi' kmaq or L'nu can be mentioned here as an example. In the form of language as stories, they create an account of life, difficulties, and precise observations of the world that surrounds them. This world includes fish, birds, trees, animals, and other life forms. Storytelling functions as education concerning how interactions with the world are shaped and how life forms are connected (Young 2018, 10).

15. Traditional Ecological Knowledge (TEK) uses the example of indigenous native peoples of North America to describe a spiritually oriented observation of nature and natural phenomena in a concept of community, practiced according to Western scientific approaches. All aspects of a physical space are capable of acting as part of the community. Animals, plants, and landforms are described as part of the community and are considered spatially and time oriented. This means, firstly, that all 'things' are interconnected, which are conceptually linked to the western community ecology. Secondly, all things are connected that have the emphasis from human to ecological community as the focus of theories about nature. Traditional ecological knowledge of indigenous cultures thus allows TEK to be linked to concepts of Western science, as these are inherently multidisciplinary and link the human and the nonhuman (Pierotti and Wildcat 2000, 1333–1335).

16. Cajete also assumes that consistent inclusion raises relevant questions about whether it is okay for animals to be bred purely for food and for hundreds of

microbes, plants, insects, and animal species to be wiped out because humans have lost their connection to the world (Cajete 2000, 153).

17. The necessity of including indigenous cultures in Multispecies Ethnography results firstly from their lifelong contact with the immediate environment and secondly from their indigenous mode of observation, which is hardly possible for researchers of Western sciences (Linkous Brown 2006, 50).

18. Using the example of 'animal-assisted services,' the triadic view clarifies a consideration of the human being, the animal deployed, and the client. It makes clear that humans, animal(s), and client(s) can interact in equal measure and that this interaction is conditional. The interaction takes place in an active form and can be characterized by two or three actors (Ameli 2016, 95). The triadic view focuses on the change of perspectives between humans, animals, and the surrounding animate and inanimate environment.

19. Haraway's expression "Make kin, not babies" means admitting relatives—outside the usual categories of kinship—based on attachment.

20. However, one challenge of the methodological implementation is that, for example, a tiger in the zoo could be degraded as an object by being photographed. This area of tension makes ethical discussions necessary in the further development of the method. Nevertheless, in the sense of an object, the possibility remains to see the world through its eyes and thus to gain subject status (Hamilton and Taylor 2017, 105).

Chapter 5

Research Design of a Multispecies Ethnography

Current research uses Multispecies Ethnography as a methodology only sporadically. This means that both the theoretical reception and a differentiated presentation of the implementation of the methodology are hardly documented. As a result, there is a lack of in-depth data on research designs of multispecies research with Multispecies Ethnography.

The following chapter will address this desideratum and, with the help of Multispecies Ethnography, trace relevant characteristics of a research design systematically and in a structured manner in order to make the "aspects of research from the minute details of data collection to the selection of data analysis techniques" (Ragin 1994, 191 cited in Flick 2010, 173) tangible. For this purpose, firstly, references to qualitative research are made and secondly, the transformative parts of the methodology are classified in greater depth. These are again not to be understood conclusively and rigidly but serve as a processual approach to a concrete (qualitative) research design in multispecies research of HumansAnimalsNaturesCultures.

A research design is fundamentally closely tied to the formulation of the research question. Multispecies ethnographic research is bound to an open attitude toward the research object. The selection of all methods used is not made in advance, but is adjusted minute by minute in the process and in the context of the research question (Thomas 2019, 33; Breidenstein et al. 2013, 51) in order to bridge the "abyss between the theoretical planned sketch and real field structure" (Benkel and Meitzler 2015, 234). This does not mean that researchers go out and research without a 'plan.' Rather, they have an overview of the research object and the research process and can thus design the procedure in a comprehensible, justifiable, and situation-specific manner. An applied ability to reflect and triangulate ensures that different perspectives are taken and one's own view is broadened. This is applied to data, methods, as well as theory (Flick 2011, 12–14).

In this chapter, the theoretical approach of HumansAnimalsNaturesCultures serves as a starting point for exemplary multispecies research with the help of Multispecies Ethnography. In the following, an analysis of teaching-learning processes in the field of nature and experiential education is traced as an example to visualize the methodology as well as the opportunities and limitations. The research design pursues a concrete investigation of complex relationships between humans and the multi-human world in teacher training. The module selected for this purpose is closely linked to sustainable educa-tion and aims to illuminate the concept of nature from a historical, cultural, and philosophical perspective for students of educational science. In addition to western scientific approaches, indigenous peoples' approaches and their indigenous knowledge of nature and animals were included. All parts were held online, with a focus on student contributions—supported by videos, essays, and online discussions. This allowed for further insights in question-ing educational processes with the more-than-human world. However, a chal-lenge arose from the fact that humans, animals, and animate and inanimate nature were primarily thematized in digital contexts, but this could be incor-porated through autoethnographic aspects in the research design. The inclu-sion of the more-than-human world in (sustainable) educational processes at universities raises questions about the meaning, roles, and social construction of the more-than-human world in these very teaching and learning pro-cesses. So far, the implementation of nature-based learning (i.e., education that recognizes the value of interaction between teachers, students, animals, and nature as intentional and non-intentional interdependence) has not been explored using multispecies analysis.

Using Multispecies Ethnography, the exemplary research design therefore specifically analyzed those interdependencies as well as the perceptions and reflections that students built up in the learning process, always relating back to the more-than-human world. The following section, however, does not refer to the results but concentrates on the methodological design of the research.

The procedure in the analysis of the interactions and relationships of students and the more-than-human world is a complex event, which is why Preuß recommends for complex objects of investigation—as is the case in the analysis of teaching and learning processes—that a well-considered and methodological indication be made, which pursues a "discovery of theory from—in social research systematically obtained and analyzed—data" (Glaser and Strauss 2005, 11). In this context, she refers to grounded theory, which was used in the aforementioned example of the chosen exem-plary analysis both for the theory-discovering qualitative methodology of

Multispecies Ethnography and for the analysis of the research question. The consideration of grounded theory is particularly interesting with regard to the further analysis of the methodology of a Multispecies Ethnography, as it is oriented toward the elaboration of a theory grounded in data in order to explain social processes (Preuß 2012, 182). The theoretical sampling in Multispecies Ethnography builds on and is related to the research question and the rationale of the approach (Thomas 2019, 34). This is based on classical ethnography.

> Theoretical sampling is a procedure 'in which the researcher decides on an analytical basis what data to collect next and where to find it.' 'The basic question in Theoretical Sampling is: which groups or subgroups of populations, events, actions (to find divergent dimensions, strategies, etc.)' does one approach next in the data collection? And what is the theoretical intention behind this? 'Consequently, this process of data collection is controlled by the evolving theory.' (Strauss 1998, 70)

It is necessary that there is an adaption to the subject area so that Multispecies Ethnography can be used to explore what role the more-than-human world actually plays in teaching-learning processes, as well as what networks emerge between human and more-than-human worlds and how these are characterized in themselves. The discovery of ongoing processes from individuals to organizations must be taken into account (Hildenbrand 2004, 32; von Kardorff 1995, 3). Here, the analysis of the research question allows multilayered insights to be drawn from different perspectives in their complexity and holism. The analysis of nature-based teaching and learning concepts hence allows for the "acting and interacting of subjects in everyday life" (Flick 2010, 27), and the recording of acting and interacting with nature and animals both within teaching/learning processes and in the research design. Investigating the network from the perspective of teachers, learners, nature, and animals allows us to analyze "ways of seeing and acting related to the object," which are linked to "different subjective perspectives and social backgrounds" (Flick 2010, 29). To grasp these connections, it is obligatory to classify the more-than-human world through individual actors in their interactions as part of this network.

5.1 SELECTION OF THE SAMPLE AND ROLE OF THE RESEARCHERS

The analysis of teaching/learning processes with the help of Multispecies Ethnography requires that one starts from a collective. Acting in a collective leads to far-reaching analyses being carried out and one or more individual cases being analyzed in detail (Breidenstein et al. 2013, 46). Acting in a collective illustrates a high degree of complexity for HumansAnimalsNaturesCultures, so that in the context of the example chosen here—despite the demand to employ Multispecies Ethnography to do so—individual subareas are only taken into account to a limited extent in the research design. Similar to qualitative interviews, it becomes apparent that in the research design presented here with the help of Multispecies Ethnography—taking into account the research question—essential subareas, such as the organization of the university or the political control of the education system, are not taken into account in detail, because an overwhelming demand on both the research design and the role of the researchers is possible. The selection hence focuses on selected actors in the sense of a micro-perspective view but retains the basic idea of taking complex interactions into account (Hildenbrand 2004, 32–33; Preuß 2012, 183). Nevertheless, this fact highlights essential challenges and limits of the methodological orientation, even though the core of Multispecies Ethnography, namely the inclusion of the more-than-human world, is consistently maintained.

Breidenstein et al. (2013, 47–48) state that ethnography in particular is suitable for practicing cross-border research. This results from the diversity of the researchers' interest in knowledge and the chosen research question with regard to the transgression of borders. Consequently, various questions and directions can be pursued in the present example. First, it can be assumed that in an education of "becomingwith" (qtd. in Haraway 2018, 12.) with animals and nature, students leave the field of the 'classroom' during the teaching/learning processes and change into an 'everyday natural living environment.' The focus on becomingwith the more-than-human world leads to questions arising for the individual and superordinate lifeworld about its effect on individual lifestyles, which are now included as part of the ethnographic analysis. A second possibility, using the example of university teaching/learning processes, also emerges in focusing on how the more-than-human world is fundamentally anchored in university curricula.

For this, it is significant to take as broad a spread as possible in order to sufficiently explain the phenomenon under investigation (Brüsemeister 2008, 173). In Multispecies Ethnography, leaving the classical field is a special feature, since nature and animals are included in the research in parts in 'other places.' This results in parallels to "multi-sited ethnography" (Ekström 2006), which follows a network of social situations (Spradley 1980, 43–45) and can also be used for the analysis of HumansAnimalsNaturesCultures.

For Multispecies Ethnography, it can therefore be assumed that a combination of academic ethnography with the function of an advocacy ethnography for animals or the entire more-than-human world emerges, which nevertheless allows for change and engages actors of the more-than-human world in an innovative way (Fetterman 2010, 134–136).

For the Multispecies Ethnography in the present example, a procedure at the interface of classical ethnography and grounded theory was carried out in the first step. Valuable insights and theories could be generated here, which were considered extremely helpful at this stage for the further development of the methodology, but also for the results of the case study on multispecies-education.

The focus on the methodology and the willingness to take on this important role as a researcher was realized in the sense of the research question. The appropriateness of the object was considered in order to enable the observation of all actors (Brüsemeister 2000, 33–35; Kelle and Kluge 1999, 15).

5.2 ETHICS OF THE RESEARCHERS

In order to adhere to good scientific practice, it is obligatory to reflect on essential ethical guidelines for humans, animals, plants and all living creatures in advance and to abide by them during the process. However, it is particularly difficult to obtain consent from nature and animals in the classical sense, so that ethical questions and unknowns always remain (Mathews and Kaltenbach 2011, 155). Nevertheless, consideration of the current ethical guidelines along with the rules of good scientific practice should be understood as a standard (Flick 2010, 56–57) when multispecies research is conducted with the help of Multispecies Ethnography. The selection of the method can include a reflective cost-benefit analysis in advance to ensure that the scientifically best possible procedure is practiced and that no other or more suitable methods are available for the research project.

The various disciplines follow different national and international codes of ethics in their research (e.g., DGS 2014, BTK n.d.; DGfE 2005; Interagency Advisory Panel on Research Ethics 2018), which ensure agreement on the adherence to standards within the fields of work, state of knowledge, methodology, and experience. They all have in common a deeper documentation of theory, methodology, and design. They, furthermore, all present in detail the findings and ways concerning the research process (DGS 2014, BTK n.d.; DGfE 2005; Interagency Advisory Panel on Research Ethics 2018). In doing so, researchers always take an objective role, which at the same time ensures respectful and appreciative interaction with all actors involved. This guarantees at all times that all persons and actors involved in the survey do not experience any disadvantages as a result of the research. An assurance prepared in advance must be made available to the participants, whether they request it or not (Brüsemeister 1997, 269). The assurance contains detailed information about what data will be collected, so that any participation is on a voluntary basis and that all relevant personal data is anonymized. In addition, information on the researchers, data storage, evaluation, and use should be included (DGS 2014). In addition to informing all those involved, the backup of the data carriers or their feeding into general data storage programs must be documented. In the EU, the GDPR must be taken into account here, as it additionally regulates the processing of personal data. In advance, any possible contact must be designed in such a way that the rules of communication, whether analogue or digital, are observed. This requires sensitivity on the part of the researchers to adjust to the respective actors and to establish a basis of trust for the research collaboration (Brüsemeister 1997, 269).

For multispecies research, the advantage of observing, consulting documents, or conducting interviews lies in the fact that the personal rights of those being studied are guaranteed at all times. Thus, actors have a free decision about what information they want to present in the interview. In addition, they can in principle dissolve or terminate the interaction at any time. All personal recordings (interviews, conversations, and videos) are transcribed anonymously. This ensures that identification with confidential information is ruled out and that personal data is adequately protected and only discussed with people involved with the project (DGS 2014).

Compared to other methods, such as the exclusive collection of interviews, the ethics of ethnographic research has a uniqueness. This results from the close relationship between researchers and participants in the field. Ambiguities about the epistemological meaning of knowledge arise from this, as the procedure in the field is often characterized by co-creation between researchers and participants. This can lead to moral dilemmas, as it is not always clear who owns the ethnographic data and researchers often claim the use of the jointly created data for themselves. In detail, this means that the data is provided by the participants and a researcher only acts as an instrument for data collection. As an example by Russell and Barley shows, this prevailing power relationship must be reflected ethically (Russell and Barley 2020, 7–8). The authors object to the fact that, after evaluation, ethnographic data from a project can be used for a political intervention program against radicalization, without those researched agreeing to this in advance.

This example makes the importance of protecting the researched actors visible, as if the matter were magnified under a burning glass. In this context, this applies especially to people "on the fringes of society" (Russell and Barley, 17). The protection has to ensure that no results are taken out of context and are falsely reproduced. It also highlights the limitations of using them for discourses of superiority or inferiority (Russell and Barley, 15) by making clear that researchers need an awareness that the data they collect does not automatically belong to them (Moodie 2010, 819). This realization consequently requires an ethical reflection on what can ultimately count as data and who speaks for whom (Denzin et al. 2017; Russell and Barley 2020). This reflection cannot be conclusively undertaken in advance but only reaches its final design in the process (Russell and Barley 2020, 4). It is clear, however, that this requires competences in moral, political, methodological, and theoretical perspectives (Russell 2005; Russell and Barley 2020, 4–5).

Russell and Barley are therefore extremely critical of the current trend of checking scientists' compliance with ethical guidelines and feeding their data into databases. The authors describe that this very development leads to scientists being exposed to pressure because they are regulated. On the other hand, the feed-in and use of data outside the research context particularly affect the basis of trust with the participants in ethnographic research projects (Russell and Barley 2020, 5–6).

The focus of the current codes of ethics shows a focus on human actors. Excluded from this are areas in which experiments are carried out with animals. Here, the ethical justifiability and the reference back to the 3Rs principle (see section 2.4.) are weighed up in the context of ethics committees and official approvals in terms of cost-benefit analysis (Biedermann 2009). The use of Multispecies Ethnography is currently not yet anchored in the codes of ethics. However, the use of the more-than-human world makes an adaptation of these ethical codes necessary. A fundamental ethical review of research projects involving humans and the more-than-human world could be carried out, as is already the case in the Anglo-American world, in order to weigh up the possible effects as well as the costs and benefits in greater depth.[1]

Last but not least, it is always advisable to reflect on how the more-than-human world is included and which ethical consideration processes are relevant. For the exemplary research project on teaching/learning processes, these balancing processes were especially produced through autoethnographic notes.

5.3 CONCEPTUALIZATION OF THE RESEARCH QUESTION

In the entire research process, the research question is of high importance for the design, the exploration of the field as well as for the case selection and data collection (Flick 2010, 132). The overarching research question in the analysis of the teaching/learning processes mentioned at the beginning focused on the question of how interdependencies between students, teachers, and the more-than-human world were shaped in university teaching/learning processes, as well as how the more-than-human world was specifically included in these processes and what role attributions were associated with this.

Research questions do not arise "out of nowhere" (Flick, 133), but are often linked to the biographical experiences and motivations of researchers. In addition, they are based on theory and analyze essential micro-areas. Although ethnographers in particular tend to want to capture the (surrounding) world in its entirety, the following applies: "A huge amount of effort is put in at the front, and only small buns come out at the back" (Thomas 2019, 35).

Deriving the research question from the problem in a theory section requires a "theoretical sensitivity" (Strauss and Corbin 1996, 25–27), which runs through the entire research process and is always checked against the appropriateness of the decisions (Flick 2010, 133). Gaps in theory are the driving force of empirical research and provide the necessary openness while at the same time practicing a clear idea of what the research should uncover. The formulation of the research question(s) thus means approaching the object of research and clarifying what is to be achieved empirically through field contact. This also includes considering which available means will be used to answer the research question(s) (Flick, 135–137).

In the context of Multispecies Ethnography, the research question in the sense of Thomas (2019, 35–36) is only considered to be completed when the research is finished. Accordingly, it is only final when all questions within the research project have been answered (Thomas, 35–36).

> How the field is circumscribed, which places and spaces are visited, which events are to be observed, which interview method is used, which people are to be spoken to, how the evaluation is carried out, what the important evaluation topics are, what the structure of the presentation of the results is; all this is clarified by recourse to the research question. (Thomas 2019, 36)

This also means that a concrete research question requires a reduction of diversity and (pre-)structures the field under investigation (Flick 2010, 134–135). However, the greatest challenge is rather to formulate the right question than to find answer(s) to this question. For this reason, it is advisable that an openness is practiced when proceeding by employing Multispecies Ethnography in order to explore all directions with the help of "generative questions" (Strauss 1998, 50) without neglecting the clarity of the research (Flick 2010, 133). Strauss and Corbin state that all undertakings must be brought together in precisely one question in order to work on the specific research project (1996, 98–99). After answering the research question, ethnographic multispecies research then ends up with its own 'small' theory (Thomas 2019, 36).

5.4 FIELD ENTRY/EXIT

One of the most important guidelines for ethnographers is: "Go into the field, look around, and collect all the data that can be of interest" (Thomas 2019, 47). Ethnography itself does not fundamentally assume a natural setting, but focuses on relevant sections of the field. Natural settings do not mean a near-natural space, but delimited social spaces characterized by social meanings, interactions, and power structures. The analysis of a limited field, however, only uncovers the visible for the researcher (Thomas 2019, 37).[2]

Qualitative (multispecies) ethnographic research processes are usually characterized by dense and intensive contacts, in which the participants are motivated to take part in the research beforehand. This demands special skills and abilities from the researchers to take on different roles and positions in the research process (Flick 2010, 142–143). This integrates the preservation of a professional foreignness (Agar 1980) and a simultaneous proximity to the field (Flick 2010, 150).

This dual role can lead to uncertainty before field entry, as plans are often contrary to reality. However, if field access is successful, the copresence of the researchers in the field creates trust and builds relationships, provided that the researchers signal an open and interested approach. The success of field access is usually not characterized by researcher's presentation of scientific details, but by their ability to adapt to the conditions of the group. One success factor here is the language of the group (Thomas 2019, 39–40). Following on from this, Lamnek (2005) has documented various roles of researchers in the research process. These illustrate the changing role of the researcher in the different phases of the research process (Mathews and Kaltenbach 2011, 155; Flick 2010, 123). What all phases have in common is that the researchers immerse themselves in the events without wanting to have a fundamental influence on them or to influence them in a particular direction. This requires a high level of acceptance and willingness to adapt on all sides (Mathews and Kaltenbach 2011, 155).

Research with the help of Multispecies Ethnography is 'unbiased'[3] in order to generate a discovering research process in which primarily the directly experienced is questioned (Mathews and Kaltenbach 2011, 155; Flick 2010, 123). For this purpose, the researched and the more-than-human world are followed into the field beyond the boundaries of organizations and places.

In doing so, it is obligatory that researchers incorporate reflexivity and openness in order to acknowledge subjectivity as part of the research process and to include all actions and impressions, such as emotions, feelings, and questions (Flick 2010, 123). Consequently, a confidence concerning their role is necessary for the researchers to be able to appear unbiased and free without neglecting the possibilities and limits in the reflection of impressions. The consideration of already-existing power positions plays a role here (Thomas 2019, 46–47), especially in the context of the inclusion of other species and natures.

Field entry necessitates that in multispecies research, in addition to gaining insights into human actors, the perspective of actors from the more-than-human world is also engaged (Fenske 2017, 22–24). For this purpose, decisions are made in the research process—with reference to spatial and temporal conditions—on how to implement the meaningful adaptation of the survey in interdependence with the characteristics and particularities of the field (Breidenstein et al. 2013, 50). In the sense of Moore and Kosut (2014), this requires an openness and attentiveness toward the actors involved, which can be characterized by a generosity of ideas and balanced by rationality and emotionality (Fenske 2017, 22–24). This openness and attentiveness is already specified in advance through autoethnographic notes and agreed upon with gatekeepers.

Access to people, groups or subareas of the more-than-human world, often requires formal consent from chairpersons or managing persons at the interface of humans and the more-than-human world (Girtler 2001, 100–102). Contacting them, for example, by phone or email, does not automatically imply the organizations' consent to a planned research project. Rather, they have "a wide range of practices at their disposal to keep curious third parties at bay, to generate information about themselves, and to control its use" (Girtler, 100–102). When analyzing an organization, it can therefore be helpful to research its organizational structures in advance and to present the announcement as plausibly and comprehensibly as possible (Girtler, 100–102). It is not uncommon for a 'gatekeeper' to prove helpful for this in the first step (Thomas 2019, 43; Breidenstein et al. 2013, 52). However, once the consent of the management level has been obtained, this does not automatically mean access to the persons or parts of the more-than-human world who are to participate in the actual survey. Rather, the trust and loyalty of the organizations or individuals must be won (Thomas 2019, 43; Breidenstein et al. 2013, 50). "Gatekeeper[s]" (Thomas 2019, 43; Breidenstein et al. 2013, 52), patrons, or sponsors can also be helpful here (Breidenstein et al. 2013, 55), as they provide access to the front stage of the field, which is extended by the researchers to access the back stages (Goffman 1959, 114). This allows for a longer stay in the field and deeper relationships (Thomas 2019, 43).

Last but not least, it must be noted that not only ethnographers (co-)draw a construction of the field, but also the researched (co-)draw a picture of the field in which they are active. In addition, an attempt is made to include the perspectives of the more-than-human world in equal measure (Breidenstein et al. 2013, 50).

Multispecies ethnography consequently constitutes itself firstly through a self-organized border formation that is temporarily opened and individually negotiated. Secondly, the tailoring of the object of the research project is realized through an analytical constitution, and the agenda is directed toward the networks in which the research is conducted. At the same time, thirdly, a process constitution takes place, which emerges in the process of access itself. The reaction to the researchers characterizes the communication context in the network (Breidenstein et al. 2010, 60).

5.5 METHODOLOGY OF MULTISPECIES ETHNOGRAPHY

Before conducting a Multispecies Ethnography, it is necessary to make a good selection of observations and to set the appropriate focus. This is what Thomas describes as "catching the phenomen[a]" (Thomas 2019, 47–48). By this, he means an explorative approach, which is highly relevant for the still relatively little-received research subject of Humans-AnimalsNaturesCultures. Explorative research projects are particularly suitable when little theoretical and reliable empirical data is available and a reconstruction of "specialized knowledge" is desired (e.g., Honer 2000). Researchers must not be afraid to formulate strong hypotheses that may be proven right or rejected in the course of the process (Honer, 51–52). For this, in the sense of Donna Haraway, all rules must be broken in order to question previous knowledge and transfer it to other species (Haraway 2018, 91–93).

The challenges in using Multispecies Ethnography can be described with John Law as follows: "Methods, their rules, and even more methods' practices, not only describe but also help to produce the reality that they understand" (Law 2004, 5). This requires concrete and innovative questioning, as only these can provide answers to the question(s) we have posed. This allows to map parts of the reality of animal and nature experience, beyond experiments and outside existing methods (Fudge 2017, 17) and to practice a "learning on the go" (Thomas 2019, 52). For Multispecies Ethnography, however, it is currently not conclusively clear whether something is actually discovered and, if so, how it is discovered. This ambiguity must be reflected upon in the research process in order to analyze what progress is made through one's own research. Only in this way can the use of methodology and the inclusion of actors from the more-than-human world be carried out in the spirit of the research question (Thomas 2019, 52). As a result, however, this means a changed perception and the multi-perspective comprehension of phenomena that may previously have been viewed from only one perspective.

In the practical implementation of a Multispecies Ethnography, it is significant that a "becomingwith, not becoming" (qtd. in Haraway 2018, 12.) concerning the more-than-human world is practiced. This means perceiving each other in a relational, material-semiotic secularization and analyzing what or who the more-than-human world is. Histories of becomingwith of actors in the more-than-human world emerge through collaborations and interdisciplinary perspectives. These allow for a transformation of previous stories and the experience of collective adventures. Through this, new stories are generated and, in turn, new perspectives. This broadening of perspective is a process that is interpreted holistically in terms of the collaborations and the observed stories and narratives of actors in the more-than-human world (Haraway, 180–182). In addition, it is possible to work with other materials that were not generated from participant observation or interviews. These include, for example, documents or videos. In this way, the complexity of social situations can be mapped even more clearly and thus a paradigm shift for alternative ways of understanding relationships with other species can be stimulated (Hamilton and Taylor 2017, 135). The inclusion of an effort to give an explicit voice to actors in the more-than-human world enables a new way of thinking (Hamilton and Taylor, 174). This poses the greatest challenge, since there is an imbalance in principle when people research other people on the one hand and the more-than-human world at the same time. Simply because understanding humans seems easier than taking a squirrel's perspective to see interdependencies.

Another example of a Multispecies Ethnography can be an analysis of the (ambivalent) human-animal relationship according to Mauss: He describes a deeper analysis using examples of hunting, the industrial processing of animals, animal experiments, or cuddling with animals. Here, all objects are to be examined in relation to the researchers themselves, to other humans, animals, the animate and inanimate environment, and in relation to actors or the observed system (Mauss 2013, 79).

This is first captured in micro-sociological terms, without ignoring complexity and interdependencies. Mauss uses the example of meal consumption to illustrate this: The type of meal, arrangement of dishes, cutlery, cuisine, preparation of the food, preservation of food, and ideological aspects of food and drinks consumed are included. For a focus on meat consumption, this means ethnographic consideration and inclusion from the moment of breeding to consumption (Mauss, 100). With regard to Multispecies Ethnography, plants, feeding places, water points, and habits of the animals would also be analyzed on the basis of location (Mauss, 105–106).

These examples already illustrate the main challenges of research technology, namely the diversity of complexity and the danger of losing the overview. Accordingly, questions must always be asked of the material in the research process in order to obtain as detailed a picture of reality as possible and to answer the where, who, when, for whom, and why (Mauss, 105–106).

In the analysis of the present material, following Mauss, further questions were also focused on that are fundamentally relevant to Multispecies Ethnography:

1. By whom is a research artifact used, with whom are actors in Humans-AnimalsNaturesCultures in relationship and in what context?
2. How do interactions between humans and actors in the more-than-human world come about and why? How are these shaped for all actors?
3. What is the purpose of the interaction/relationship?
4. Is its use general or specific? (Maus 2013, 73–74).

The analysis with the help of Multispecies Ethnography also requires a quantum of intuition. Thus, it is not sufficient to focus only on rationality, as especially the understanding that comes from 'inside out' offers today's human-animal-nature research in the cultural and social sciences initial points of contact (see also Köchy et al. 2016; Kaldewey 2008).

5.6 DOCUMENTATION OF ETHNOGRAPHIC MULTISPECIES RESEARCH

For the documentation of ethnographic multispecies research, it is advisable to keep a research diary (Atteslander 2003, 110), as data only emerges if experiences, impressions, and statements are recorded (Breidenstein et al. 2013, 86; Thomas 2019, 96). Hence, individual partial documentations do not occur, as Thomas (2019, 110) recommends. Rather, all content and documents are collected and documented in a common document. This means not only taking written notes of direct observations but also transcribing audio and video excerpts (Thomas, 92).[4] Thomas (2019, 105–106) and Fetterman (2010, 83–85) describe various pieces of equipment that are necessary for a successful documentation of ethnographic research. These include:

- Notebook or sketchpad
- Portable PC or smartphone
- Audio recorder
- (Film) camera or disposable cameras
- Handheld scanner

Various forms of protocols that systematically outline the research process are used to track the appropriateness of the individual research steps

(Brüsemeister 2008, 81). According to Lofland et al. (2006, 111), for every hour spent in the field, one hour of writing should be assumed for documentation in the follow-up. This should be done with a clear head, if possible, so that no essential parts are lost. Ideas, intermediate hypotheses, methodological reflections, and feelings are noted down and subdivided on the basis of observational, methodological, and theoretical notes (Brüsemeister 2008, 82). This results in a documentation of actions and interactions for the contextual enrichment of statements or ways of acting (Flick 2010, 371).

1. Observation notes describe a verbatim reproduction and description of the observed situation by means of written or technical records. Here, all observations, impressions, and experiences made during the observation period are documented (Brüsemeister 2008, 82; Hohmann 2012, 67; Breidenstein et al. 2013, 86). The combination of written and auditory recordings allows descriptions of nonverbal events to be combined with those of snapshots. Both the long-term perspective and conceptualization are included without omitting complex events and over-complex material (Breidenstein et al. 2013, 87).
2. Theoretical notes refer to further observations in the context of assembling the collected data and the theoretical links to the aforementioned observation notes. These allow the creation of intermediate hypotheses for subsequent observations and the entire research process (Brüsemeister 2008, 82). Text artifacts in particular provide good insights for theoretical notes and analysis (Breidenstein et al. 2013, 87).
3. Methodological notes describe the reflexive control of one's own procedure and allow the research design to be repeatedly adapted and further developed in the context of the research question (Brüsemeister 2008, 82).
4. Memos are descriptive memory notes that accompany the entire research process—from data collection to data analysis. Here, it is important to ensure that the respective references to the exact text passages are presented in the notes (Thomas 2019, 111–112).

The forms of documentation follow a holistic approach that depicts symbols and rituals of HumansAnimalsNaturesCultures and their conceptualization through an empirical perspective and multiple realities. Here, not only inter- and intra-cultural diversity is taken into account but also their structures and functions on micro and macro levels. Last but not least, the forms of documentation allow for operationalizability (Fetterman 2010, 83–85).

The collection of data can be realized through text documents and audio or video recordings as well as documentations of event sequences. Notes make capturing the volatility of the events and connecting them to the researcher's memory possible. They, therefore, support the researcher in reconstructing the course of events to a later time (Breidenstein et al. 2013, 86).

The collection of data in the example of the analysis of teaching/learning processes described at the beginning results from multispecies ethnographic observations of the module as well as the essays of diverse research work of the students on nature-based and sustainable learning with actors of the more-than-human world (in pedagogical contexts). In addition, a research diary with all relevant data was prepared. In the present research design, this included videos, texts, documentations, and films. The complex collection allowed for in-depth observation and analysis as well as precise documentation of all external and autoethnographic data, experiences, and feelings.

There are different views on the timing of appropriate logging. While Breidenstein et al. (2013, 97–98) assume that the essential notes should be taken on the basis of one's memory when seated at the desk, Thomas (2019, 106) argues that memory sketches should already be made in the field. He supports his point with Goffman's (1996, 267) assumption that breaks would always be available to note down relevant results, although this would have to be assessed situationally (Thomas 2019, 106–107). Particularly in the case of participant observation in the context of multispecies research, however, it should be noted that the researcher may not have time for a piece of paper and pen, as they are busy perceiving all impressions. It is nevertheless suggested that documentation be made promptly after leaving the field, as everything is still "fresh" (Breidenstein et al. 2013, 97). In addition, it is recommended for Multispecies Ethnography to include textual artifacts, such as written researcher accounts, to support observations and findings.

In this respect, Multispecies Ethnography has another special feature, namely that the previous "people writing" becomes "people writing about animals and nature" (Hamilton and Taylor 2017, 196). David Abram also points to this in his work 'The Spell of the Sensuos' (Abram 1996, 263). Here, he assumes that human communities would benefit from the textual competences of the intimate and reciprocal relationship between humans and nature, since language functions not only intra- but also inter-specifically (Abram 1996, 116–117).

Therefore, the special feature of multispecies ethnographic field notes is that they are in part only comprehensible to the respective researchers themselves, since essential emotions and sensations are included in the protocol forms.

The aforementioned forms of recording (observation notes, theoretical and methodological notes) serve the researchers as a reminder of observations made (Breidenstein et al. 2013, 86–87). However, they also enable intersubjective verifiability, which is a central quality criterion (see chapter 7). This refers less to a 'correct' reproduction of an observation note than to how it interacts with theoretical and methodological notes. This includes whether the meaning of an observation note could not only have occurred 'naturalistically' in the field, but whether the meaning of an observation note was fully developed and interpreted through theoretical and methodological notes. This can be seen in the amount of notes alone, whereby beginners tend to note the least when taking methodological notes (Brüsemeister 2008, 32–34).

When researchers enter the field, they often have little knowledge of what to expect. This is particularly relevant in the context of the transformation toward ethnographic multispecies research. For this reason, it is advisable, especially at the beginning, to focus on initial impressions in all facets and with all senses, because all details are important. Special attention should be paid to the researched (Breidenstein 2013, 89), the more-than-human world, and their 'expressions.'

For this reason, it can be helpful to record sounds and images in order to conduct a focused and repetitive observation. This helps the medium of the body in the field to balance the limited observational capacity. Recording allows for a focus on sensations or body language areas in order to match them with the active communication gestures at a later stage (Breidenstein et al. 2013, 89–90).[5]

Writing down all impressions, emotions, and observations is a relevant storage process that elicits the explication of tacit knowledge in detail (Breidenstein et al., 96). This step is very labor-intensive if it is to be achieved that anonymous readers can follow the explanations. It is therefore better to describe too much than too little (Breidenstein et al., 97). Using the example of participant observation, a documentation of a small, concentrated sequence will illustrate this. This was created during a previous ethnographic analysis. Over a period of 18 months, observations were repeatedly carried out with a trained dog. Elderly people were visited on a residential ward to find out the effects of animal interactions on the life satisfaction of the residents of a senior citizens' facility.

> At the next visit, she already shows more interest. She watches the dog and the researcher shows her the treats. With the help of the researcher, she gives the dog treats. While doing so, she does not say a word. She looks very interested and almost inviting, which prompts the researcher to give her more treats. She feeds the dog with the researcher's help until she loses concentration after a while. When she turns away, the researcher ends the interaction. The researcher remains seated with Ms. West. Meanwhile, Ms. West repeatedly seeks eye contact by smiling and looking invitingly. (Hohmann 2012, 96; name anonymized)

Although readers get a good idea of what happened from this brief snippet of description, this microscopic section is a thinned out version of a rich description and particularly highlights the focus on the human actors (as envisaged in the research design). Following the Multispecies Ethnography, the earlier section should be updated with a sharpened focus on the dog and its point of view to clarify the protocol forms and documentation in the form of a differentiated description:

> During the next visit, Ms. West already shows more interest and this can also be observed with dog Enzo. He moves freely and, starting from himself, seeks contact with Ms. West. She observes Enzo closely—in a slightly bent-forward posture—as he looks her in the eye. Both observe each other and the researcher is excluded from the previously triadic interaction for a short period of time. Thus, for a moment, there is only a direct interaction between Ms. West and Enzo, resulting from both actors looking at each other and minimal changes in their postures. This can be seen in Ms. West's smile and in the fact that she leans forward, while Enzo, ears facing forward, looks at her.

The dyadic interaction is interrupted when Enzo looks at the researcher and then takes in the hand with the treats. The researcher talks to the dog and agrees with Miss West to put treats in her hand. The communication is completely nonverbal, as Miss West does not speak a word. The dog eats the treats from Miss West's hand, then runs to a plant and sniffs it. Meanwhile, Miss West looks very interested and almost inviting, which prompts the researcher to give her more treats. Doing so, the researcher talks to her, glancing at Enzo at the same time. He comes back after a few minutes and eats the treats from Miss West's hand until she loses concentration after a while. When she turns away, the researcher ends the interaction. Enzo, on the other hand, still briefly tries an approach by licking Miss West's hand. Then he runs around the room until he finally lies down.

The researcher stays with Miss West and talks to her about what has happened. Meanwhile, Miss West repeatedly seeks eye contact, she smiles, and looks back and forth between the researcher and Enzo (adapted from Hohmann 2012, 96; name anonymized).

Dense descriptions are helpful for the implementation of analyses of HumansAnimalsNaturesCultures, whereby in this example, the emotional area of the researcher was completely excluded from the description. However, the analysis of the same in the constructed setting has put the perspective on all three actors. This implies that the impressions and free encounters basically make it possible to classify the value and meaning of the interactions professionally, ethically, and scientifically.

This means that an "accurate and detailed account of what is experienced" (Thomas 2019, 101) is undertaken without abandoning scientific claims to knowledge. Thomas thus contradicts Gobo and Molle (2017, 196–198) and Breidenstein et al. (2013, 101) in arguing to reduce protocols. The author takes a critical stance on the transfer from thin to dense descriptions in the context of ethnographic analysis, as the description and the protocol should already be so rich that they would not be further condensed in the analysis (Thomas 2019, 104). This approach can also be cited for Multispecies Ethnography. This means that recording and organization are already sufficiently documented in the research design. Not least because the descriptions are processed analytically. It must be taken into account here that these are already selective and interpretative per se, since they take place within social interactions (Breidenstein et al. 2013, 102–103; Schatzmann and Strauss 1973, 94; Emerson et al. 1995, 8). Precise writing down and documenting already represents a first analytical step in the further in-depth evaluation. The emergence of analytical notes, which are referred to as "by-products of descriptive work" (Breidenstein et al. 2013, 104), also plays a role here. They provide recurring analytical models, theoretical concepts, and explications of results that allow rich descriptions (Thomas 2019, 99) and are integrated into the further evaluation.

5.7 EVALUATION

The evaluation of multispecies ethnographic research is currently not uniformly regulated, neither is it described in depth, which is why it is first derived on the basis of the evaluation methodology of classical ethnography.

The basis of data evaluation describes tools given by perceiving, active listening, "reading, thinking and writing" (Thomas 2019, 115), which draw on the material in retrospect to draw conclusions about the reality under investigation. For this either "a synthetic condensation of situation descriptions or an analytical dissection of the data" (Thomas 2019, 115) is carried out. An analytical evaluation of multispecies ethnographic data follows the sequencing, coding, and subsequent categorization so that it can be ordered in the form of a theory (Thomas, 116). Synthetic analysis, on the other hand, is not infrequently carried out through dense descriptions. This procedure, also named rich description (Thomas 2019, 102), is applied in the field of market research, for example, and is carried significantly through three areas: Culture, language, and context.

a. Culture describes a structured behavior of a specific group to which a particular meaning is attached. Culture is closely related to identity, which, however, is not rigid but is constantly redefined through recurring behavior. This means, for example, that consumption or the interaction with

nature is always interpreted against the cultural background (Mathews and Kaltenbach 2011, 153).
b. Language represents an ethnographic object of study in order to get closer to a culture. Language can therefore be identified in ethnographic analyses, especially in human-animal interactions, as a boundary to be crossed. This does not only result from the different ways of expression; even the interpretation of language is perceived differently. Language must therefore be analyzed against the background of individual values, expectations, and different situational conditions (Mathews and Kaltenbach, 153–154). Daly and Caputi basically assume a positive meaning of language in ethnography (Daly and Caputi 1987, 18), which is adapted for Multispecies Ethnography. For this purpose, it can be helpful in some places to change the meaning of a word or to combine it with other words in order to form new meanings (Daly and Caputi, 169).
c. Context can range from situational conditions to character traits, culture, and history. Ethnographic observations must take into account the overall context of the observation and are to be placed in this context (Mathews and Kaltenbach 2011, 154).

Consequently, dense descriptions pursue three functions in the analysis of data: documenting, explicating, and communicating (Breidenstein et al. 2013, 106). In the example of the aforementioned analysis of teaching/learning processes, a hybrid of synthetic and analytical procedures emerged. Thus, the evaluation logic could initially use dense descriptions, whereby parts of these descriptions were already available as learning reports. For this reason, a research diary with all relevant data was prepared in preparation for further evaluation. In the present research design, this included videos, texts, documentations, and films. The complex collection enables both in-depth observation and analysis as well as the precise documentation of all external and autoethnographic data, experiences, and feelings. The documentation and writing down of relevant findings, coupled with the available documents— so-called analytical notes—already represent in themselves a first analytical step that generates ideas and prepares the systematic analysis of the data (Thomas 2019, 102–104).

In addition to the consideration of the dense descriptions, the planned project followed the systematic collection of all data for the analytical theory generation of nature-based online learning at a university. For this purpose, a deeper elaboration of a theory of nature-based online learning was carried out with the help of grounded theory. This was preceded by the concrete selection of the research location, the agreed cooperation of the researchers, and a change of the researcher's entire center of life in order to implement a Multispecies Ethnography in another country and within the framework of digital teaching/learning formats for the planned research question. grounded theory describes an object-anchored theory that undertakes inductive analysis. Data collection, analysis, and theory are seen and analyzed in changing interdependence (Strauss and Corbin 1996, 7–8).

The prevalence of creativity in the research process, which is elementary for Multispecies Ethnography in particular, allows one to "aptly label categories, let one's mind wander, form free associations necessary for asking stimulating questions, and make comparisons that lead to new discoveries" (Strauss and Corbin 1996, 12). The categories described in this process represent relevant theoretical elements for the conceptual elaboration of the theory (Glaser and Strauss 2005, 45), but have been repeatedly validated in the ongoing research process. Here, in addition to the consideration of the research question(s), a background knowledge of the field as a whole plays a role, although this must not restrict researchers in the formation of ideas, evaluation, and theory generation (Strauss and Corbin 1996, 12–13). Induction, deduction, and hypothesis generation are thus combined (Kelle and Kluge 1999, 21–22).

A theory generation of 'medium scope' represents a process that is situated between working hypotheses and all-encompassing theories (Glaser and Strauss 2005, 30–32). To elaborate this theory, compliance with four essential criteria is necessary: Consistency, Comprehensibility, Generality, and Control (Glaser and Strauss, 227–229). This enables "a series of procedures [to develop] inductive, derived object-anchored theories about a phenomenon" (Strauss and Corbin 1996, 8). This way, the object is not only developed in its interdependence, but it is tested at the same time (Strauss and Corbin, 9–10).

grounded theory hence enables the development of a theory based on data, which is elaborated processually in the context of conditions, strategies, and consequences (Gessner 2014, 6; Hülst 2010, 281). The reconstructive evaluation results from the background of existing scientific models, which enable the in-depth description of the research object in order to substantiate the theory in the research itself (Gessner 2014, 7; Böhm 1994, 122–123).

Here, the theoretical sampling described by Strauss and Corbin (1996, 148) was also implemented by collecting, coding, and analyzing the data simultaneously (Glaser and Strauss 2005, 54). This step, in the analysis of the entire teaching/learning process, made generating a theory and synthesizing it abstractly, while maintaining theoretical sensitivity (Glaser and Strauss, 54) and using the various categories, possible (Gessner 2014, 9; Glaser and Strauss 2005, 47–49).

Theory formation has already taken place in the research process through recurring questions about the material (Strauss 1991, 70), by searching for categories (Kelle and Kluge 2010, 48) and relating them to each other until a theoretical saturation is reached (Strauss and Corbin 1996, 159).

Within the framework of the analysis, codes were first used to deconstruct the data (Brüsemeister 2008, 157), whereby dimensions of categories emerged and commonalities and differences were presented. This led to an interlocking of open and axial coding (Strauss and Corbin 1996, 76). The choice of codes affected the categories that followed.

The importance of grounded theory emerged in this example through the analysis of nature-based online learning, where documents and existing models of 'nature and outdoor learning' were considered. These form the conditions within the status of research and allow for adaptation and alignment with the theory being developed. Here, the data was aligned and meshed with the theory to provide a structured and meaningful picture of the prevailing teaching/learning processes.

The results showed a changed view of the world through the inclusion of nature in the gradation of learning about nature, online learning about and with nature, learning with media and nature, and learning from nature (Ameli 2020).

NOTES

1. The exemplary research design was reviewed by an external ethics committee.

2. An attempt to remove these limitations is carried out with multisited ethnography, whose approaches can also be made tangible for Multispecies Ethnography (Ekström 2006), since with Multispecies Ethnography, the mutual influence between humans, natures, animals, and cultures, as well as these as a unit, is taken into account.

3. Kassam points out that researchers can never be unbiased observers of our natural world because they participate in the world and with the world. This participation is characterized by relationships with other humans, nonhuman life such as plants or animals, and their inanimate environment. This means that they are always involved in research through their bodies and their thoughts, because relationships have a decisive influence on knowledge (Kassam 2009, 89).

4. For transcripts, it can be recommended to write down what was said according to the rules of medium accuracy as it was spoken (see in detail Brüsemeister 2008, 131–132; Fuchs-Heinritz 2000, 271–273; Breidenstein et al. 2013, 91–92).

5. Here, Breidenstein et al. (2013, 89) note that a camera only captures concentrated and fixed points of view, while research generates complementary and different insights through roaming gazes, zooming, and tactile experiences.

Chapter 6

Quality Criteria of Multispecies Research

Although they are highly relevant for the quality of the results (Thomas 2019, 5), the quality criteria of qualitative research are currently not conclusively established (Flick 2010, 487). According to Flick (2010, 487–489) and Thomas (2019), at least three perspectives on quality criteria can be identified, First, the application of quality criteria from standardized research to all research results of quantitative methods; second, the application of special quality criteria only to qualitative research; third, a mix of both. This third approach is adopted for Multispecies Ethnography.

The various methodological orientations and approaches of Multispecies Ethnography require adherence to quality criteria that assess whether the chosen methodological decisions and procedures have been empirically implemented in a manner appropriate to the subject matter and whether a differentiation of the descriptions made has been observed (Thomas 2019, 54; Breidenstein et al. 2013, 184).

Multispecies Ethnography—like classical ethnography—does not pursue statistical representativeness, but an open and multi-perspective view of HumansAnimalsNaturesCultures (Thomas 2019, 54; Breidenstein et al. 2013, 184).

For this, Steinke (1999, 324) describes intersubjectivity as an essential quality criterion. Intersubjectivity, as comprehensible documentation of presuppositions, experiences, and theories, provides clarity about the object of research and enables outsiders to understand the processuality of what is happening and to judge its appropriateness (Thomas 2019, 54). Intersubjectivity refers to a construction, deconstruction, as well as structured and reconstructed interaction in complex systems (Jackson 1998, 8; Madden 2017, 24). It is thereby paradoxical and ambiguous in nature (Jackson 1998, 8). This poses a challenge, as it does not operate in stable constitutions between the I and the You (Madden 2017, 25). This creates pitfalls, indeterminacies, and ambiguities for Multispecies Ethnography, which are overcome through intersubjectivity. Mauss suggests implementing intersubjectivity through a value-freedom and without anger or wonder in the research process (Mauss 2013, 47–49).[1]

In general, the trust of academia in ethnography exists when it is scientifically well implemented (Madden 2014, 281) and the process of transformation is recognizable. This is tied to valid, reliable, and accurate research (Kompatscher et al. 2017, 207). For Multispecies Ethnography, reliability in qualitative research refers to the quality of the recordings and documentation of the data. In order to increase reliability, these should be documented in as standardized a manner as possible—especially in interdisciplinary research associations—in order to increase comparability (Flick 2010, 490). Here, the credibility of the narrator plays a crucial role and is challenging because the documentation of nature and animal encounters or interactions with actors of the more-than-human world are difficult to order in their complexity (Adams et al. 2019, 10).

Consequently, the discussion goes "towards an explication in two respects" (Adams et al., 10). This requires, firstly, that verifiability becomes clear via the observations and statements of the research subjects and the interpretation of the researchers. Secondly, the procedure in the field is made explicit in order to make the differences between researchers visible. Finally, the reflexive documentation of the research process should increase reliability. One way of implementing this is communicative validation (Flick 2010, 494–495), which describes a correspondence with the participants from the field and their perspective on the research object. However, Breidenstein et al. (2013, 1986) see this critically, as they assume that participants are mostly "poor commentators of their practice" (Breidenstein et al. 2013, 186). Last but not least, communicative validation through the peer review of participants can lead to the premature termination of fieldwork (Breidenstein et al., 186). The difference in the view of the researcher and the researched rather describes an essential quality feature of "going native," in which neutrality and quality are required (Breidenstein et al., 187–188).

Another characteristic of qualitative research is validity. Here, the researchers' construction of the research object and the construction of the researched are thought through (Flick 2010, 494–495). According to Breidenstein et al. (2013, 184), data in ethnography could hardly be valid, as it would only become analyzed data through the researchers' sense-making. This would often cast doubt on the controllability of the data, because social processes are mixed with their interpretation. At the same time, the authors describe precisely this criticized flexibility and intensity in research processes as a procedure to dissolve the prevailing methodological constraints (Breidenstein et al., 185).

For this reason, Madden understands validity as a plausibility and conclusiveness of the story, the experiences made, impressions, and conclusions, which are to be documented in such a way that they are as connectable as possible. This includes all methodical and methodological reflections with regard to the influence of ethnographers (Madden 2014, 20, 282).

For Multispecies Ethnography, it can be stated with Wolcott (1990, 127–128) that the assurance of validity is guaranteed by the following characteristics:

- Close listening to the researcher in the field
- Accurate and early recording
- Data presented in such a way that it is possible for readers to understand and draw conclusions from it
- Data presented openly and completely and a balance maintained between different aspects without losing accuracy (Flick 2010, 497)

Validation therefore concerns the entire research process, from data collection to the presentation of results (Flick, 498).[2]

According to Madden, objectivity as the third criterion of qualitative research is insufficiently discussed, since research directions and the understanding of reality vary from researcher to researcher. In Madden's sense, a first step consists of a detailed description as well as a systematic collection of data, the systematic penetration of the data and the adequate processing and presentation of the data. The stringent implementation allows—despite the strong structuring—room for experimental and inventive approaches (Madden 2014, 282). Nevertheless, the problem with the normativity of qualitative research is primarily described in the fact that both the research practice and the generation of theory do not happen objectively. Rather, they are subjectively classified in historical and cultural contexts (Ahrens et al. 2008).

Quality assurance for multispecies ethnographic research hence represents a challenge that needs to be further developed through regular debates and discourses (Flick 2010, 50).[3] Following Steinke (1999, 326–328), Thomas (2019, 56–58) therefore refers to current debates on the reliability of collected ethnographic data. These are also mentioned by Madden (2017, 25–26) and consequently presented for Multispecies Ethnography:

1. *Appropriateness of the research question:* Data reliability can only be achieved if an adequate research question has been formulated, which is constantly reflected upon and reviewed during the research process. Although the complexity of the empiricism is consciously included, it is

nevertheless conceptualized in the research question. Here, in the sense of Thomas, a sensitivity must be maintained that makes it possible to map central dimensions of the research object and the reference back to scientific theories (Thomas 2019, 56; Breidenstein et al. 2013).

2. *Appropriateness of the research design:* The research design should—even if ethnography has a variety of possibilities—already be specified in parts in order not to run the risk of practicing arbitrariness or non-specificity. This does not mean that researchers cannot use the variety of methods in ethnographic research. Rather, it focuses on the triangulation of methods, theories, cases, and data in order to connect the diversity of perspectives (Flick 2010; Thomas 2019, 57).

    A central subarea is the research diary (see section 5.6), which allows for a subjective reflection of the attribution processes of the research field and for checking the quality of the research design. Reflective questions should always be asked here: Which natural processes are outside the field and thus remain unconsidered? Which micro-view is included? Which approaches to HumansAnimalsNaturesCultures open up to me as a researcher and which do not? What role do ethnographers play in this network? Which blind spots remain undiscovered? (Thomas 2019, 58)

3. *Appropriateness of data collection:* The choice of methodology should not follow personal preferences, but should be based on the theoretical sampling and the selected objects of investigation. It should be noted that the question of what exactly is to be analyzed and what the next steps are should be included. The appropriateness of data collection goes hand in hand with the formulation of the research question and makes it possible to compare the advantages and disadvantages of possible methods. Here, an "interplay of decentering and recentering is necessary" (Thomas 2019, 58–59). The quality of the appropriateness is checked by relevant questions. These include questions on theoretical sampling as well as reflection on the balance in the interplay of proximity and distance (Thomas, 58–59).

4. *Adequacy of data documentation and processing:* The documentation and processing of the collected data requires a regulated recording through objectified approaches (Flick 2010; Thomas 2019, 59). These have been described in section 5.6 and illustrate the effectiveness and benefits for the research as a whole. The focus is on the question of whether the documentation of the data was carried out appropriately and whether the significance and meaningfulness were taken up in a differentiated manner (Thomas 2019, 59–60).

For research using Multispecies Ethnography, this means that the quality criteria are elicited and balanced through reflexive questions throughout the research process:

1. Does the account of multispecies-ethnographic research show sufficient interdependencies and encounters between humans, animals, and natures, and can these be represented and comprehended using the example of a particular technique?
2. Are the relationships between the actors involved described in an understandable and comprehensible way?
3. Is the complexity of the process depicted and is its direction of action—in relation to the research question—recognizable?
4. Is a point of view outside the representation taken into account and reflexively processed?
5. Does the more-than-human world or its actors come into their own, to be sufficiently included in the representation and the change of perspective? Is the participation and appreciation of species that are not directly involved in the interactions taking place?
6. Can the feasibility of the interaction be replicated in principle and integrated into a research process?

Finally, validity in generalization becomes more important. In this context, it is essential to strive for a fit in theory-practice transfer. Consequently, density and systematics play a decisive role in order to be able to form conclusive derivation statements based on the data basis. Here, generalizations are to be formulated on an empirical basis which, through a conceptual level, ensure that the subject matter is broken down theoretically. The range and variance also play a role, as constant comparisons with existing theories and comparable cases allow the theory to be formed in the first place. Ultimately, this step follows the questions of ensuring the chosen evaluation methods and their relevance to the content of theory building (Thomas 2019, 61).

NOTES

1. Pitfalls, indeterminacies, and ambiguities are not meant to disguise the volatility, ambiguity, and relationality of multispecies encounters, nor are differences between species to be ignored (Madden 2014). Mauss also states that human-animal-nature relations are not automatically one-sided and asymmetrical, but diverse and multi-perspectival. Using the example of the taming of a dog by humans and the taming of humans by cats, he illustrates that there are species-different effects and forms of relationships between humans and animals (Mauss 2013, 29–30).

2. Validity is characterized by Aikenhead and Mitchell in indigenous worldviews as time plus survival (Aikenhead and Michell 2011, 89).

3. Ethnographic research, and especially autoethnography, is often critiqued for its nonscientific nature. The lack of theoretical analysis in particular leads to a naïve and emotional view, resulting in distorted realities. This happens above all because the

duties of hypothesizing, analyzing, and theorizing are not fulfilled. This criticism is increasingly found in natural science research, which also refers to the lack of criteria, although these do not explicitly exist for autoethnography. Even though emotions are described as a major point of criticism in ethnographic analyses, it is striking that this criticism is very extensively manifested in emotional criticism of researchers (Adams et al. 2019, 11–13).

Chapter 7

Conclusion

The advent of posthumanism offers new opportunities and possibilities for including the more-than-human world in (interdisciplinary) research projects by deconstructing symbols, discourses, and institutional segments of the category 'human' (Pedersen 2011b, 67). The analyses of complex HumansAnimalsNaturesCultures attached to this require a holistic approach and an interdisciplinary cooperation of different disciplines, without losing qualities of the different specializations of the disciplines. The multiple crises of the 21st century already clearly demonstrate that the existing and future problems are more far-reaching than any single discipline or methodology can capture (Hamilton and Taylor 2017, 167–169). As a result, difficult questions are solved more comprehensively in an interdisciplinary team than alone. Interdisciplinary research on HumansAnimalsNaturesCultures allows the boundaries of humans and the more-than-human world to become more permeable in research contexts and thus generate new, innovative, and inter-related insights. Linked to this is a specialization of the scientific disciplines involved, which, with simultaneous interdisciplinary opening, enables a reciprocal reference and stimulates and proactively takes up the reflection of identities in the network of relationships. This results in new perspectives and transformative developments in scientific understanding and the use of estab-lished routines and methods, which initiate a change in the view of actors of the more-than-human world as coresearchers.

In order to holistically consider research on the diverse and ambivalent contact zones of humans and the more-than-human world, it must first be taken into account that the further apart disciplines are, the more complex the organization of research projects and the risk of failure becomes (Sukopp 2010, 15–16; Bendix and Bizer 2011, 1–3). This results from the different cultures and languages in the respective disciplines. However, these can be loosened by methodological and theoretical interdisciplinary approaches and, in the sense of Heckhausen (1987), result in a "composite interdisciplinarity" in the first step. Here, initially "neither the subject areas of the respective subjects (. . .) nor their methods or theoretical levels of integration" overlap (Jungert 2010, 5). Only in the second step does this very interdisciplinary cooperation practice result in a fusion of methodology and solution of tasks from different perspectives through border crossings (Jungert 2010, 8).

In its methodological approach, the (interdisciplinary) orientation in the analysis of HumansAnimalsNaturesCultures allows the more-than-human world to participate in research processes and hence promises new theoretical and empirical insights that allow existing concepts to be revised, questioned, and supplemented. This is closely linked to Bendix and Bizer's thesis that the global world society needs to focus more on interdisciplinary research in the future (Bendix and Bizer 2011; Bendix et al. 2017).

In conclusion, Multispecies Ethnography can be described as a hybrid research methodology that allows for analyses of HumansAnimalsNaturesCultures.

Multispecies Ethnography describes an ethnographic methodology that observes and reflects on educational and research processes of humans and actors of the more-than-human environment. The methodology offers a perspective to understand animals and natures as social actors of the more-than-human world with agency and hence as subjects in scientific research. It is therefore about the transformation process of a so-called object of science toward a subject in the interdisciplinary research process.

Consequently, the aim of Multispecies Ethnography is also to stimulate the reflective capacity of researchers, lecturers, and students, as well as to further develop methodology in the long term in order to renew research and teaching processes (Hamilton and Taylor 2017, 104). Multispecies Ethnography thus integrates how scholarship is practiced and communicated, research emerges, and ultimately knowledge is created through research and educational processes. It extends this through the participatory inclusion of the more-than-human world.

Multispecies Ethnography follows a hybrid form in a participatory research style. Here, humans, animals, and nature are understood as coresearchers and are allowed to participate in society and in research processes (von Unger 2013, 1). Multispecies Ethnography hence requires a high degree of flexibility if a high value is placed on the participation of the more-than-human world. This implies perceiving multispecies research as a holistic approach that analyzes multispecies relationships and relations in greater depth. The inclusion of hybrid approaches in the methodological orientation allows a transformation of research methods and the disciplines in multispecies research to approach a common denominator (Hamilton and Taylor 2017, 157). In particular, the combination of qualitative and quantitative research[1] appears necessary both to generate far-reaching insights and to allow the boundaries between social and natural sciences to become more permeable and to permit hybrid research.

In the sense of Latour (1995), Schulz understands hybridization as something that is characterized by bodies, senses, and a scattering of impressions (Schulz 2015, 52) as well as by thinking, feeling, and despairing (Hamilton and Taylor 2017, 148). This hybridization makes social worlds possible. Their insights take on a high significance for the daily relationships and contact zones of humans, animals, and natures (Hamilton and Taylor 2017, 164).

The interdisciplinary and multi-perspective analyses require combining old theories with new insights and relating them from different (inter-) disciplinary perspectives. At this very point, it (still) remains open what the consequences are if approaches used from the different disciplines cannot be combined with each other (Kompatscher et al. 2017, 26) or how the coexistence of representation and perception as well as the blurring of dichotomies is implemented (Haraway 2008, 4).

It is also questionable whether researchers show differences in the representation of a dog, an earthworm, a bird, or a woodlouse, for example. Consequently, for the future practice of Multispecies Ethnography in hybrid participatory approaches, it remains unclear how these will be concretely implemented in disciplinary and interdisciplinary research fields. This is to be further concretized in future multispecies research. This includes questioning the view of actors in the multispecies world, the scientific understanding, and the use of established routines and methods.

The introduction of a Multispecies Ethnography is a bridge for methodological and theoretical (ethnographic) analyses of different disciplines. It is implemented positivistically, innovatively, cautiously, and reflexively and allows for multiple perspectives.

NOTE

1. For more information on mixed methods see Kuckartz (2017), Baran (2020).

Works Cited

Abels, Heinz. 2007. *Interaktion, Identität, Präsentation: Kleine Einführung in die interpretativen Theorien der Soziologie*. Wiesbaden: VS Verlag für Sozialwissenschaften.

Abram, David. 1996. *Spell of the Sensuous*. New York: Random House.

Abram, David. 2010. *Becoming Animal*. New York: Random House.

Absolon, Kathleen E. (Minogiizhigokwe). 2011. *Kaandossiwin: How We Come to Know*. Halifax/Winnipeg: Fernwood Publishing.

Adams, Tony E., Stacy Holman Jones, and Carolyn Ellis. 2015. *Autoethnography*. New York: Oxford University Press.

Adams, Tony E., Carolyn Ellis, Arthur P. Bochner, Andrea Ploder, and Johanna Stadlbauer. 2019. "Autoethnografie in der Psychologie." In *Handbuch Qualitative Forschung in der Psychologie*, edited by Günter Mey and Katja Mruck, 1–22. Wiesbaden: Springer.

Agar, Michael H. 1980. *The Professional Stranger*. New York: Academic Press.

Ahrens, Johannes, Raphael Beer Uwe H. Bittlingmayer Jürgen Gerdes, eds. 2008. *Beschreiben oder Bewerten: Normativität in ausgewählten sozialwissenschaftlichen Forschungsfeldern*. Vol. 1. Münster: VS-Verlag für Sozialwissenschaften.

Aikenhead, Glen and Herman Michell. 2011. *Bridging Cultures: Indigenous and Scientific Ways of Knowing Nature*. Toronto: Pearson.

Albert, Mathias, Klaus Hurrelmann, Gudrun Quenzel, Ulrich Schneekloth, and Ingo Leven. 2019. *Jugend 2019 – 18. Shell Jugendstudie: Eine Generation meldet sich zu Wort*. Weinheim: Beltz.

Alger, Janet M. and Steven F. Alger. 2003. *Cat Culture: The Social World of a Cat Shelter*. Philadelphia: Temple University Press.

Alverdes, Friedrich. 1952. *Tiersoziologie: Forschungen zur Völkerpsychologie und Soziologie*. Vol. 1. Leipzig: C. L. Hirschfeld.

Ameli, Katharina. 2016. *Die Professionalisierung tiergestützter Dienstleistungen: Von der Weiterbildung zum eigenständigen Beruf*. Bielefeld: wbv.

Ameli, Katharina, Anja S. Dulleck, and Thomas Brüsemeister, eds. 2016. *Grundlagen tiergestützter Dienstleistungen: Tiergestützte Therapie, Pädagogik und Fördermaßnahmen als interdisziplinäres Arbeitsfeld.* Hamburg: tredition.

Ameli, Katharina and Christopher Hühn. 2016. "Unterrichtsgestaltung mit Tieren in der Grundschule." In *Grundlagen tiergestützter Dienstleistungen: Tiergestützte Therapie, Pädagogik und Fördermaßnahmen als interdisziplinäres Arbeitsfeld*, edited by Katharina Ameli, Anja S. Dulleck, and Thomas Brüsemeister, 385–396. Hamburg: tredition.

Ameli, Katharina. 2020. *Where is the Nature in Nature and Outdoor Learning?* Unpublished manuscript. Sydney.

American Veterinary Medical Association and One Health Initiative Task Force. 2008. "One Health: A New Professional Imperative." Schaumburg, IL: AMVA. Accesssed August 1, 2019. https://www.avma.org/KB/Resources/Reports/Documents/onehealth_final.pdf

Anderson, Eugene N. 2011. "Ethnobiology: Overview of a Growing Field." In *Ethnobiology*, edited by Eugene N. Anderson, Deborah M. Pearsall, Eugene S. Hunn, and Nancy J. Turner, 1–14. New Jersey: Wiley-Blackwell.

AnimalHealthEurope. 2017. "One Health." Accessed October 1, 2019. https://www.bft-online.de/fileadmin/bft/pressemitteilungen/12-10-2017/One_Health_Grafik.jpg

Arantes, Lydia M. and Elisa Rieger. 2014. "Einleitung." In *Ethnographien der Sinne. Wahrnehmung und Methode in empirisch-kulturwissenschaftlichen Forschungen*, edited by Lydia M. Arantes and Elisa Rieger, 13–20. Bielefeld: transcript.

Arluke, Arnold. 1993. "Associate Editor's Introduction: Bringing Animals into Social Scientific Research." *Society and Animals* 1: 5–7.

Arluke, Arnold and Clinton Sanders. 1996. *Regarding Animals.* Philadelphia: Temple University Press.

Arluke, Arnold, Jack Levin, Carter Luke, and Frank Ascione. 1999. "The Relationship of Animal Abuse to Violence and Other Forms of Antisocial Behavior." *Journal of Interpersonal Violence* 14 (9): 963–975.

Atkinson, Paul, Amanda Coffey, Sara Delamont, John Lofland, and Lyn Lofland. 2001. *Handbook of Ethnography.* Los Angeles et al.: SAGE Publications.

Atteslander, Peter. 2003. *Methoden der empirischen Sozialforschung.* Rieden: de Gruyter.

Baran, Mette L. 2020. *Applied Social Science Approaches to Mixed Methods Research.* Hershey: IGI Global.

Barraza, Laura and Isabel Ruiz-Mallén. 2017. "The 4D's: A Pedagogical Model to Enhance Reasoning and Action for Environmental and Socio-Scientific Issues." In *Envisioning Futures for Environmental and Sustainability Education*, edited by Arjen E. J. Wals, Joseph P. Weakland, and Peter Blaze Corcoran, 257–269. Wageningen: Wageningen Academic Publishers.

Barth, Matthias, Jasmin Godemann, Marco Rieckmann, and Ute Stoltenberg. 2007. "Developing Key Competencies for Sustainable Development in Higher Education." *International Journal of Sustainability in Higher Education* 8 (4): 416–430.

Bath, Alistair J. and Joy W. Enck. 2003. "Wildlife-Human Interactions in National Parks in Canada and the USA." All U.S. Government Documents. (Utah Regional Depository) Accessed January 17, 2017. http://digitalcommons.usu.edu/govdocs /424

Becker, Egon. 2016. *Keine Gesellschaft ohne Natur: Beiträge zur Entwicklung einer sozialen Ökologie.* Bad Langensalza: campus.

Bekoff, Marc. 2004. "Wild Justice and Fair Play: Cooperation, Forgiveness, and Morality in Animals." *Biology and Philosophy* 19: 489–520.

Bell, Michael M. 2012. *An Invitation to Environmental Sociology.* Los Angeles et al.: SAGE Publications.

Bendix, Regina and Kilian Bizer. 2011. *Verbundförderung für interdisziplinäre Gesellschafts- und Kulturwissenschaften: Eine Kritik.* Göttingen: Cultural Property Policy Papers 3 of the Göttingen Interdisciplinary Research Group on Cultural Property.

Bendix, Regina F., Kilian Bizer and Dorothy Noyes. 2017. *Sustaining Interdisciplinary Collaboration. A Guide for the Academy.* Illinois: University of Illinois Press.

Benkel, Thorsten and Matthias Meitzler. 2015. "Feldforschung im Feld der Toten: Unterwegs in einer Nische der sozialen Welt." In *Wege ins Feld: Methodologische Aspekte des Feldzugangs*, edited by Angelika Poferl and Jo Reichertz, 234–251. Essen: Oldib-Verlag.

Berg, Eberhard and Martin Fuchs, eds. 1993. *Kultur, soziale Praxis, Text: Die Krise der ethnographischen Repräsentation.* Frankfurt a. M.: Suhrkamp.

Berger, Peter L. and Thomas Luckmann. 1980. *Die gesellschaftliche Konstruktion der Wirklichkeit.* Frankfurt a. M.: S. Fischer.

Bergmann, Jörg. 2008. "Medienethnographie." In *Handbuch Medienpädagogik*, edited by Uwe Sander, Friederike von Gross, and Kai-Uwe Hugger, 328–334. Wiesbaden: VS für Sozialwissenschaften.

Berkes, Fikret, Johan Colding, and Carl Folke. 2000. "Rediscovery of Traditional Ecological Knowledge as Adaptive Management." *Ecological Applications* 10 (5): 1251–1262.

Bertelsmann Stiftung and Sustainable Development Solutions Network (SDSN). 2018. *SDG Index and Dashboards Report 2018.* New York: Bertelsmann Stiftung/ SDSN.

Biedermann, Maria. 2009. *Überwachung und Kontrolle genehmigungspflichtiger Tierversuche vergleichend in Deutschland und Großbritannien.* Berlin: Mensch und Buch Verlag.

Binder, Regina. 2007. "Der 'vernünftige Grund' für die Tötung von Tieren." *Natur und Recht* 29: 806–813.

Bläske, Alexandra. 2019. *Tierschutzaspekte bei der privaten Haltung von und dem Handel mit (exotischen) Säugetieren in Deutschland.* PhD diss., University of Munich.

Blattner, Charlotte E. 2019. "Rethinking the 3Rs: From Whitewashing to Rights." In *Animal Experimentation: Working Towards a Paradigm Change*, edited by Kathrin Herrmann and Kimberley Jayne, 168–193. Leiden: Brill Human-Animal-Studies Series.

Block, Katharina. 2016. *Von der Umwelt zur Welt: Der Weltbegriff in der Umweltsoziologie.* Bielefeld: transcript.

Blumer, Herbert. 1997. "Forward." In *Violent Criminal Acts and Actors Revisited,* edited by H. Lonnie and L. Athens Urbana, 1-6. IL: University of Illinois Press.

Blumer, Herbert. 2013. *Symbolischer Interaktionismus.* Translated by Michael Dellwing and Viola Abermet. Berlin: Suhrkamp.

Bögeholz, Susanne. 1999. *Qualitäten primärer Naturerfahrung und ihr Zusammenhang mit Umweltwissen und Umwelthandeln.* Opladen: VS Verlag für Sozialwissenschaften.

Böhm, Andreas. 1994. "Grounded Theory: Wie aus Texten Modelle und Theorien Gemacht Werden." In *Texte verstehen. Konzepte, Methoden, Werkzeuge,* edited by Andreas Böhm, Andreas Mengel, and Thomas Muhr, 121–140. Konstanz: Universitätsverlag.

Boellsdorf, Tom. 2008. *Coming of Age in Second Life.* New Jersey: Princeton University Press.

Bohnsack, Ralf. 1997. "Adoleszenz, Aktionismus und die Emergenz von Milieus: Eine Ethnographie von Hooligan-Gruppen und Rockbands." *Zeitschrift für Sozialisationsforschung und Erziehungssoziologie* 17 (1): 3–18.

Boll, Tobias. 2019. *Autopornografie: Eine Autoethnografie mediatisierter Körper.* Bielefeld: transcript.

Bollig, Sabine and Sascha Neumann. 2011. "Die Erfahrung des Außerordentlichen: Fremdheit/Vertrautheit als methodisches Differential einer Ethnographie pädagogischer Ordnungen." *Zeitschrift für qualitative Forschung* 12 (2): 199–216.

Bonz, Jochen. 2014. "'Im Medium der eigenen Menschlichkeit...': Erläuterungen und Beispiele zum ethnopsychoanalytischen Ethnografieverständnis, das im Feldforschungsprozess auftretende Irritationen als Daten begreift." In *Alltag–Kultur–Wissenschaft: Beiträge zur Europäischen Ethnologie,* edited by Burkhart Lauterbach, 35–60. Würzburg: Königshausen and Neumann.

Bosch, Matilda von and William Bird. 2018. "Setting the Scene and How to Read the Book." In *Oxford Textbook of Nature and Public Health: The Role of Nature in Improving the Health of a Population,* edited by Matilda von Bosch and William Bird, 3–10. Glasgow: Oxford Press.

Bourdieu, Pierre. 2005. *Das Elend der Welt.* Konstanz: UTB.

Brämer, Rainer. 2006. *Natur obskur: Wie Jugendliche heute Natur erfahren.* Munich: oekom.

Brand, Karl-Werner. 2014. *Umweltsoziologie. Entwicklungslinien, Basiskonzepte und Erklärungsmodelle.* Weinheim/Basel: Beltz Juventa.

Brand, Karl-Werner and Heino Stöver. 2008. "Umweltbewegung (inkl. Tierschutz)." In *Die sozialen Bewegungen in Deutschland seit 1945: Ein Handbuch,* edited by Rolans Roth and Dieter Rucht, 219–244. Frankfurt a. M./New York: Campus.

Brand, Karl-Werner and F. Reusswig. 2020. "Umwelt." In *Lehrbuch der Soziologie,* edited by Hans Joas, 557–575. Frankfurt a. M./New York: Campus.

Brantz, Dorothee and Christoph Mauch. 2010. "Das Tier in der Geschichte und die Geschichte der Tiere." In *Tierische Geschichten: Die Beziehung von Mensch und Tier in der Kultur der Moderne,* edited by Dorothee Brantz and Christoph Mauch, 7–16. Paderborn: Schöningh.

Braun, Annette. 2000. *Wahrnehmung von Wald und Natur.* Wiesbaden: VS Verlag für Sozialwissenschaften.

Breidenstein, Georg. 2006. *Teilnahme am Unterricht: Ethnographische Studien zum Schülerjob.* Wiesebaden: VS Verlag für Sozialwissenschaften.

Breidenstein, Georg, Stefan Hirschauer, Herbert Kalthoff, and Boris Nieswand. 2013. *Ethnography: Die Praxis der Feldforschung.* Konstanz: UTB.

Breuer, Franz, Petra Muckel, Barbara Dieris. 2019. *Reflexive Grounded Theory: Eine Einführung für die Forschungspraxis.* Heidelberg: Springer.

Brock, Anje and Julius Grund. 2018. "Bildung für nachhaltige Entwicklung in Lehr-Lernsettings. Quantitative Studie des nationalen Monitorings." Accessed August 29, 2019. https://www.bneportal.de/sites/default/files/downloads/Nationales%20Monitoring_Quantitative%20Studie_LehrerInnen.pdf

Brüsemeister, Thomas. 1997. *Leiden gleich Lernen?: Empirische und theoretische Zusammenhänge am Beispiel biographischer Entscheidungen ostdeutscher Erwachsener.* PhD diss., University of Hagen.

Brüsemeister, Thomas. 2000. *Qualitative Forschung: Ein Überblick.* Wiesbaden: Westdeutscher Verlag.

Brüsemeister, Thomas. 2008. *Qualitative Forschung: Eine Einführung. Ein Überblick.* Wiesbaden: VS Verlag für Sozialwissenschaften.

Brundiers, Katja and Arnim Wiek. 2011. "Educating Students in Real-World Sustainability Research: Vision and Implementation." *Innovative Higher Education* 36 (2): 107–124.

Bryant, Clifton. 1979. "The Zoological Connection." *Social Forces* 58: 399–421.

Buber, Martin. 1999. *Ich und Du.* Gütersloh: Gütersloher Verlagshaus.

Buchner-Fuhs, Jutta. 1999. "Das Tier als Freund: Überlegungen zur Gefühlsgeschichte im 19. Jahrhundert." In *Tiere und Menschen: Geschichte und Aktualität eines prekären Verhältnisses*, edited by Paul Münch and Rainer Walz, 275–294. Paderborn: Schöningh.

Budde, Jürgen. 2015. "Reflexionen zur Bedeutung von Handlung und Praktik in Ethnography." *Zeitschrift für qualitative Forschung* 1: 7–24.

Budde, Jürgen and Michael Meier. 2015. "Ethnographie und ihre Erkenntnispotentiale: Methodische Reflexionen." *Zeitschrift für qualitative Forschung* 1: 3–6.

BTK (Bundestierärztekammere.V.). n.d. "Ethik-Kodex der Tierärztinnen und Tierärzte Deutschlands." Accessed June 6, 2020. https://www.bundestieraerztekammer.de/btk/ethik/

Bundesverband für Tiergesundheit e.V. 2017. "One Health: From Vision to Action." *Pressrelease.* Accessed August 2, 2019. https://www.bft-online.de/pressemitteilungen/one-health-from-vision-to-action/

Buschka, Sonja, Sonja Gutjahr, and Sebastian Marcel. 2012. "Gesellschaft und Tiere: Grundlagen und Perspektiven der Huma-Animal Studies." *Politik und Zeitgeschichte* 62: 20–27.

Buschka, Sonja and Jasmine Rouamba. 2013. "Hirnloser Affe? Blöder Hund? 'Geist' als sozial konstruiertes Unterscheidungsmerkmal." In *Gesellschaft und Tiere: Soziologische Analysen zu einem ambivalenten Verhältnis*, edited by Birgit Pfau-Effinger and Sonja Buschka, 23–56. Wiesbaden: Springer.

Cajete, Gregory. 2000. *Native Science. Natural Laws of Independence*. Santa Fee: Clear Light Publisher.

Cajete, Gregory. 2006. "Western Science and the Loss of Natural Creativity." In *Unlearning the Language of Conquest: Scholars Expose Anti-Indianism in America*, edited by Four Arrows (a.k.a. Jacobs, D.T.), 247–259. Austin: University of Texas Press.

Callon, Michal. 1987. "Society in the Making: The Study of Technology as a Tool for Sociological Analysis." In *The Social Construction of Technological Systems: New Directions in the Sociology and History of Technology*, edited by Wiebke E. Bijker, Thomas P. Hughes, and Trevor J. Pinch, 82–103. Cambridge, MA: The MIT Press.

Catton, William R. 1972. "Sociology in an Age of Fifth Wheels." *Social Forces* 50: 436–447.

Charmaz, Kathy. 1983. "The Grounded Theory Method: An Explication and Interpretation." In *Contemporary Field Research: A Collection of Readings*, edited by R. M. Emerson, 109–125. Prospect Heights: Waveland.

Chimaira Arbeitskreis. 2011. "Eine Einführung in gesellschaftliche Mensch-Tier-Verhältnisse und Human-Animal Studies." In *Über die gesellschaftliche Natur von Mensch-Tier-Verhältnissen*, edited by Chimaira Arbeitskreis für Human-Animal Studies, 7–42. Bielefeld: transcript.

Cobern, William W. 2000. *Everyday Thoughts About Nature*. Boston, MA: Kluwer Academic.

Cohn, Ruth C. and Christina Terfurth, eds. 2007. *Lebendiges Lehren und Lernen: TZI macht Schule*. Stuttgart: Klett-Cotta.

Coles, Alf, Justin Dillon, Marina Gall, Kate Hawkey, Jon James, David Kerr, Janet Orchard, Celia Tidmarsh, and Jocelyn Wishart. 2017. "Towards a Teacher Education for the Anthropocene." In *Envisioning Futures for Environmental and Sustainability Education*, edited by Arjen E. J. Wals, Joseph Weakland, and Peter Blaze Corcoran, 77–85. Wageningen: Wageningen Academic Publishers.

Crutzen, Paul J. 2000. "Geology of Mankind." *Nature* 415: 23.

Crutzen, Paul J. and Eugene Stoermer. 2002. "The Anthropocene." *Global Change Newsletter* 41: 17–18.

Cyrulnik, Boris, Karine L. Matignon, and Frédéric Fougea. 2003. *Tiere und Menschen: Die Geschichte einer besonderen Beziehung*. Munich: Knesebeck.

Daheim, Hansjürgen. 1969. "Soziologie der Berufe." In *Handbuch der empirischen Sozialforschung*, edited by René König, 358–399. Stuttgart: Ferdinand Enke Verlag.

Daheim, Hansjürgen. 1991. "Zum Stand der Professionssoziologie." In *Erziehen als Profession*, edited by Bernd Dewe, Wilfried Ferchhoff, and Frank-Olaf Radtke, 21–35. Wiesbaden: Leske + Budrich.

Dalke, Karen and Harry Wels. 2016. "Ethnographic Research in a Changing Cultural Landscape." In *Affect, Space and Animals*, edited by Jopi Nyman and Nora Schuurman, 181–195. London: Routledge.

Daly, Mary. 1984. *Pure Lust. Elemental Feminist Philosophy*. New York: HarperCollins.

Daly, Mary and Jane Caputi. 1987. *Websters' First Intergalactic Wickedary of the English Language*. Boston: Beacon Press.

Daumiller, Martin. 2017. *Motivation von Wissenschaftlern in Lehre und Forschung: Struktur, Eigenschaften, Bedingungen und Auswirkungen selbstbezogener Ziele*. Wiesbaden: Springer.

Degue, Sarah and David Dilillo. 2009. "Is Animal Cruelty a 'Red Flag' for Family Violence?: Investigating Co-occurring Violence towards Children, Partners, and Pets." *J Interpers Violence*. Jun; 24 (6): 1036–1056. DOI: 10.1177/0886260508319362.

Delamont, Sara. 2012. *Ethnographic Methods in Education*. Los Angeles et al.: SAGE Publications.

Dellwing, Michael and Robert Prus. 2012. *Einführung in die interaktionistische Ethnographie. Soziologie im Außendienst*. Wiesbaden: Springer.

Denzin, Norman K., Yvonna S. Lincoln, and Linda Tuhiwai Smith, eds. 2008. *Handbook of Critical and Indigenous Methodologies*. Thousand Oaks: SAGE Publications.

Denzin, Norman K. and Yvonna S. Lincoln. 2017. "Introduction: The Discipline and Practice of Qualitative Research." In *Handbook of Qualitative Research*, edited by Yvonna S. Lincoln and Norman K. Denzin, 1–26. Thousand Oaks: SAGE Publications.

Denzin, Norman K. 2017. "Critical Qualitative Inquiry." *Qualitative Inquiry* 23 (1): 8–16.

Derrida, Jacques. 2002. "Das Tier, welch ein Wort! Können sie leiden?: Über die Endlichkeit, die wir mit Tieren teilen." In *Mensch und Tier: Eine paradoxe Beziehung*. Accompanying book to the exhibition, edited by Stiftung Deutsches Hygiene-Museum, 190–208. Ostfildern-Ruit: H. Cantz Verlag.

Despret, Vinciane. 2004. "The Body We Care For: Figures of Anthropo-Zoo-Genesis." *Body and Society* 10 (2/3): 111–134.

DgfE (GERA: German Educational Research Association). 2005. "Ethik-Rat und Ethikkodex der DgfE." Accessed June 15, 2020. https://www.dgfe.de/service/ethik -rat-ethikkodex.html

DGS (Deutsche Gesellschaft für Soziologie). 2014. "Ethik-Kodex der Deutschen Gesellschaft für Soziologie (DGS) und des Berufsverbandes Deutscher Soziologinnen und Soziologen (BDS)." Accessed June 22, 2020. https://bds-soz .de/BDS/fachgruppen/ethik/Ethik-Kodex_Satzung_141003.pdf

Dierauer, Urs. 1999. "Das Verhältnis von Mensch und Tier im griechisch-römischen Denken." In *Tiere und Menschen: Geschichte und Aktualität eines prekären Verhältnisses*, edited by Paul Münch and Rainer Walz, 37–85. Paderborn: Schöningh.

Digital Nature Group. n.d. Accessed August 8, 2020. https://digitalnature.slis.tsukuba .ac.jp/

Dilly, Marc and Andrea Tipold. 2014. "Etablierung eines Skills Labs in der Tiermedizin in Deutschland." *GMS Zeitschrift für Medizinische Ausbildung* 31 (2): 1–13.

Dörhöfer, Steffen. 2003. "Die Sirenen der Aufklärung: Horkheimer und Adorno." In *Ökologische Theorien: Fünfzehn Vorlesungen zur Einführung: Kritische Philosophie, Umweltsoziologie, poetische Ausgänge*, edited by Andreas Nebelung, 34–49. Berlin: Focus.

Doolittle, Amity A. 2010. "The Politics of Indigeneity: Indigenous Strategies for Inclusion in Climate Change Negotiations." *Conservation and Society* 8 (4): 286–291.

Dooren, Thom van and Vinciane Despret. 2018. "Evolution: Lessons from Some Cooperative Ravens." In *The Edinburgh Companion to Animal Studies*, edited by Lynn Turner, Ron Broglio, and Undine Sellbach, 160–180. Edinburgh: University of Edinburgh.

Deutsche UNESCO-Kommission. nd. "Bildung für nachhaltige Entwicklung." Accessed July 5, 2016. http://www.bne-portal.de/de/bundesweit/das-weltaktion-sprogramm-deutschland

Dunayer, Joan. 2001. *Animal Equality: Language and Liberation*. Derwood/ Maryland: Ryce Publishing.

Dunlap, Riley E. 2011. "Aktuelle Entwicklungen in der nordamerikanischen Umweltsoziologie." In *Handbuch Umweltsoziologie*, edited by Matthias Groß, 54–72. Wiesbaden: Springer.

Eisenstein, Herbert. 1999. "Mensch und Tier im Islam." In *Tiere und Menschen: Geschichte und Aktualität eines prekären Verhältnisses*, edited by Paul Münch and Rainer Walz, 121–145. Paderborn: Schöningh.

Ekström, Karin M. 2006. "The Emergence of Multi-sited Ethnography in Anthropology and Marketing." In *Handbook of Qualitative Research Methods in Marketing*, edited by Russell W. Beld, 497–508. Cheltenham: Edward Elgar Publishing.

Ellgring, Heiner. 1984. "Ethologie." In *Geschichte der Psychologie: Ein Handbuch in Schlüsselbegriffen*, edited by Helmut E. Lück, Rudolf Miller, and Wolfgang Rechtien, 211–217. Munich: Urban & Schwarzenberg.

Ellis, Carolyn. 1999. "Heartful Autoethnography." *Qualitative Health Research* 9 (5): 669–683.

Ellis, Carolyn. 2004. *The Ethnographic I: A Methodological Novel About Autoethnography*. WalnutCreek: AltaMira Press.

Ellis, Carolyn and Arthur P. Bochner. 2000. "Autoethnography, Personal Narrative, Reflexivity." In *Handbook of Qualitative Research*, edited by Norman K. Denzin and Yvonna S. Lincoln, 733–768. Thousand Oaks: SAGE Publications.

Emerson, Robert M., Rachel I. Fretz, and Linda L. Shaw. 1995. *Writing Ethnographic Fieldnotes*. Chicago: University of Chicago Press.

Erikson, Erik H. 1968. *Kindheit und Gesellschaft*. Stuttgart: Klett.

Eriksen, Thomas H. 2001. *Small Places, Large Issues. An Introduction to Social and Cultural Anthropology*. London: Pluto Press.

FAO, WHO, OEI, UN System Influenza Coordination, UNICEF, and The World Bank. 2008. "Contributing to One World, One Health: A Strategic Framework for Reducing Risks of Infectious Diseases at the Animal–Human–Ecosystems Interface." Accessed August 1, 2019. http://www.oie.int/downld/AVIAN %20INFLUENZA/OWOH/OWOH_14Oct08.pdf

Fehrle, Johannes, Rüdiger Heinz, and Kerstin Müller. 2010. "Wissenschaftliche Möglichkeiten und ethische Grenzen. Die Biologie in der gesellschaftlichen Diskussion." In *Herausforderung Biologie: Fragen an die Biologie. Fragen aus der Biologie*, edited by Johannes Fehrle, Rüdiger Heinz, and Kerstin Müller, xi–xviii. Berlin: LIT.

Fenske, Michaela. 2016. "Andere Tiere, andere Menschen, andere Welt?" In *Den Fährten folgen: Methoden interdisziplinärer Tierforschung*, edited by Forschungsschwerpunkt 'Tier – Mensch – Gesellschaft', 293–310. Bielefeld: transcript.

Fenske, Michaela. 2017. "Der Stich der Biene: Multispecies-Forschung als methodische Herausforderung." *Kuckuck. Notizen zur Alltagskultur* 32–17 (02): 22–25.

Fetterman, David M. 2010. *Ethnography: Step-by-Step*. Los Angeles et al.: SAGE Publications.

Finke, Peter. 2014. *Citizen Science: Das unterschätzte Wissen der Laien*. Munich: oekom.

Flick, Uwe. 2010. *Qualitative Sozialforschung: Eine Einführung*. Reinbek: Rowohlt.

Flick, Uwe. 2011. *Triangulation: Eine Einführung*. 3rd ed. Wiesbaden: VS-Verlag für Sozialwissenschaften.

Foster, Charles. 2016. *Being a Beast: An Intimate and Radical Look at Nature*. London: Profile Books.

Fuchs-Heinritz, Werner. 2000. *Biografische Forschung: Eine Einführung in Praxis und Methoden*. Wiesbaden: VS-Verlag für Sozialwissenschaften.

Fudge, Erica. 2017. "What was It Like to be a Cow? History and Animal Studies." In *Oxford Handbook of Animal Studies*, edited by Linda Kalof, 258–278. New York: Oxford Handbooks.

Gandy, Matthew. 2019. "Marginalia: Ästethik Ökologie und städtisches Brachland." In *NaturenKulturen: Denkräume und Werkzeuge für neue politische Ökologien*, edited by Friederike Gesing, Michi Knecht, Michael Flitner, and Katrin Amelang, 139–174. Bielefeld: transcript.

Gebhard, Ulrich. 2013. *Kind und Natur. Die Bedeutung der Natur für die psychische Entwicklung*. Wiesbaden: Springer.

Geertz, Clifford. 1990. *Die künstlichen Wilden: Der Anthropologe als Schriftsteller*. Munich: Carl Hanser.

Geimer, Alexander. 2011. "Autoethnography/Performance Ethnography: Trend, Turn oder Schisma in der qualitativen Sozialforschung?" *Zeitschrift für qualitative Forschung* 12 (2): 299–320.

Geiger, Theodor. 1931. "Das Tier als geselliges Subjekt." *Forschungen zur Völkerpsychologie und Soziologie* 10: 283–207.

Gesing, Friederike, Michi Knecht, Michael Flitner, and Katrin Amelang. 2019. "NaturenKulturen-Forschung: Eine Einleitung." In *NaturenKulturen: Denkräume und Werkzeuge für neue politische Ökologien*, edited by Friederike Gesing, Michi Knecht, Michael Flitner, and Katrin Amelang, 7–50. Bielefeld: transcript.

Gessner, Susann. 2014. *Politikunterricht als Möglichkeitsraum: Perspektiven auf schulische politische Bildung von Jugendlichen mit Migrationshintergrund*. PhD diss. Schwalbach/Ts.: Wochenschau Verlag.

Gibney, Elizabeth. 2020. "Coronavirus Lockdowns Have Changed the Way Earth Moves." *Nature* 580: 176–177.

Gieryn, Thomas F. 2006. "City as Truth-Spot: Laboratories and Field-Sites in Urban Studies." *Social Studies of Science* 36 (1): 5–38.

Girtler, Roland. 2001. *Methoden der Feldforschung*. Vienna: Böhlau.

Glaser, Barney G. and Anselm L. Strauss. 2005. *Grounded Theory: Strategien Qualitativer Forschung*. Bern: Huber.

Glock, Hans-Johann. 2016. "Wann ist ein Tier ein Tier?: Zum Tierbegriff in Philosophie und Biologie." In *Tierisch! Das Tier und die Wissenschaft: Ein Streifzug durch die Disziplinen*, edited by Meret Fehlmann, Margot Michel, and Rebecca Niederhauser, 13–22. Zürich: Vdf.

Gmeiner, Martina. 2003. *Kinder an die Macht: Ängste, Sorgen, Perspektiven der Kinder*. Österreichische Kinderfreude, Vienna: Kinderfreunde.

Gobo, Giampietro and Andrea Molle. 2017. *Doing Ethnography*. London: SAGE Publications.

Goffman, Erving. 1959. *The Presentation of Self in Everyday Life*. New York: Anchor Books.

Goffman, Erving. 1974. *Das Individuum im öffentlichen Austausch: Mikrostudien zur öffentlichen Ordnung*. Frankfurt a. M.: Suhrkamp.

Goffman, Erving. 1996. "Über Feldforschung." In *Kommunikative Lebenswelten: Zur Ethnographie einer geschwätzigen Gesellschaft*, edited by Hubert Knoblauch, 261–269. Konstanz: UVK.

Gräsel, Cornelia. 2002. "Umweltbildung." In *Handbuch Bildungsforschung*, edited by Rudolf Tippelt, 675–689. Opladen: VS-Verlag für Sozialwissenschaften.

Groß, Matthias. 2006. *Natur*. Bielefeld: transcript.

Grümer, Karl-Wilhelm. 1974. *Techniken der Datensammlung 2: Beobachtungen*. Leipzig: B.G. Teubner.

Grund, Julius and Anje Brock. 2018. "Bildung für nachhaltige Entwicklung in Lehr-Lernsettings: Quantitative Studie des nationalen Monitorings." Accessed August 29, 2019. https://www.bneportal.de/sites/default/files/downloads/Nationales%20Monitoring_Quantitative%20Studie_Junge%20Menschen.pdf

Gutjahr, Julia and Marcel Sebastian. 2014. "Die vergessenen 'Anderen' der Gesellschaft." In *Einleitung: Ambivalenzen in der Gesellschafts-Tier-Beziehung*, edited by Birgit Pfau-Effinger and Sonja Buschka, 57–72. Opladen: Springer.

GV-SOLAS (Gesellschaft für Versuchstierkunde). 2013. "Die Entwicklung der Versuchstierkunde." Accessed October 7, 2019. http://www.gv-solas.de/index.php?id=18

Haan, Gerhard de. 1999. "Zu den Grundlagen der 'Bildung für nachhaltige Entwicklung' in der Schule." *Unterrichtswissenschaft* 3: 252–280.

Haan, Gerhard de. 2012a. "Geschichte der Bildung für eine nachhaltige Entwicklung." *Virtual Academy Sustainability*. Course: Education for Sustainable Development. Accessed March 3, 2017. http://www.vabne.de/index. php/de/veranstaltungen/10 0-bildung-fuer-nachhaltige-entwicklung/historische-wurzeln-der-bne/243-entw icklungspolitische-bildung

Haan, Gerhard de. 2012b. Rio+20 Summit. "Wo bleibt die Bildung?" *ÖkopädNEWS 231, Working Group Nature and Environmental Education*: 37–38.

Haan, Gerhard de. 2015. "Die UN-Dekade BNE: Bilanz einer Bildungsreform." In *UN-Dekade mit Wirkung: 10 Jahre 'Bildung für nachhaltige Entwicklung' in Deutschland*, edited by Deutsche UNESCO-Kommission, 10–17. Bonn: Deutsche UNESCO-Kommission e.V.

Hacking, Ian. 2000. "How Inevitable Are the Results of Successful Science?" *Philosophy of Science* 67: 58–71.

Halbmeyer, Ernst. 2010. "Globale Welt und Multi-Sited Ethnography." In *Einführung in die empirischen Methoden der Kultur- und Sozialanthropologie*, edited by Ernst Halbmeyer. Vienna: Universität Vienna. https://www.univie.ac.at/ksa/elearning/cp/ksamethoden/ksamethoden-84.html

Hallmann, Sylke, Christian Klöckner, Ulrike Kulmann, and Anja Beisenkamp. 2005. "Freiheit, Ästhetik oder Bedrohung?" *Umweltpsychologie* 9 (2): 88–108.

Hamilton, Lindsay and Nik Taylor. 2013. *Animals at Work: Identity, Politics and Culture in Work with Animals*. Leiden/Boston: Brill.

Hamilton, Lindsay and Nik Taylor. 2017. *Ethnography after Humanism: Power, Politics and Methods in Multi-Spezies-Research*. London: Palgrave.

Hammersley, Martyn. 2006. "Ethnography: Problems and Prospects." *Ethnography and Education* 1 (1): 3–14.

Haraway, Donna. 2008. *When Species Meet*. Minneapolis: University of Minnesota Press.

Haraway, Donna. 2018. *Unruhig bleiben: Die Verwandtschaft der Arten im Chthuluzän*. Translated by Karin Harrasser. Frankfurt: Campus.

Harmon, David. 2002. *In Light of Our Differences: How Diversity in Nature and Culture Makes us Human*. Washington, DC: Smithsonian Institution Press.

Harmon, David and Jonathan Loh. 2018. "Congruence between Species and Language Diversity." In *The Oxford Handbook of Endangered Languages*, edited by Kenneth L. Rehg and Lyle Campbell, 659–682. Oxford: Oxford University Press.

Harris, Tracey. 2017. "The Problem is Not the People, It's the System: The Canadian Animal-Industrial Complex." In *Animal Oppression and Capitalism*, edited by David Nibert, 56–75. Munich: Praeger.

Hart, Roger. 1979. *Children's Experience of Place*. New York: Irvington Publishers/Halsted Press.

Hart, Roger. 1982. "Wildlands for Children: Consideration of the Value of Natural Environments in Landscape Planning." *Landschaft und Stadt* 14: 34–39.

Hasemann, Klaus. 1964. *Verhaltensbeobachtung und Verhaltensbeurteilung in der psychologischen Diagnostik*. Berlin: Hogrefe.

Hastedt, Sabine. 2011. "Die Wirkungsmacht konstruierter Andersartigkeit: Strukturelle Analogien zwischen Mensch-Tier-Dualismus und Geschlechterbinarität." In *Human-Animal Studies: Über die gesellschaftliche Natur von Mensch-Tier-Verhältnissen*, edited by Chimaira Arbeitskreis für Human-Animal Studies, 191–214. Bielefeld: transcript.

Haubenhofer, Dorit and Inge A. Strunz. 2013. *Raus auf's Land: Bauernhöfe als zeit-gemäße Erfahrungs- und Lernorte für Kinder und Jugendliche.* Baltmannsweiler: Schneider Verlag Hohengehren.

Hauff, Volker. 1987. *Unsere gemeinsame Zukunft: Brundlandt-Bericht der Weltkommission für Umwelt und Entwicklung.* Greven: Eggenkamp.

Have, Paul ten. 2004. *Understanding Qualitative Research and Ethnomethodology.* London: New Dehli.

Hebel, Kai. 2003. "Die Umwelt der Systeme: Niklas Luhmann." In *Ökologische Theorien: Fünfzehn Vorlesungen zur Einführung: Kritische Philosophie, Umweltsoziologie, poetische Ausgänge*, edited by Andreas Nebelung, 102–119. Berlin: Focus.

Heckhausen, Heinz. 1972. "Discipline and Interdisciplinarity." In *Interdisciplinary. Problems of Teaching and Research in Universities*, edited by L. Apostel, G. Berger, A. Briggs, and G. Michaud. Paris: Organisation for Economic Co-Operation and Development (OECD).

Heidenmann, Frank. 2011. *Ethnologie: Eine Einführung.* Göttingen: Vandenhoeck & Rupprecht.

Heinämäki, Leena. 2009. "Protecting the Rights of Indigenous Peoples – Promoting the Sustainability of the Global Environment?" *International Community Law Review* 11: 3–68.

Henderson, Bob and Tom G. Potter. 2011. "Outdoor Adventure Education in Canada: Seeking the Country Way Back In." *Canadian Journal of Environmental Education* 6: 225–242.

Hersch-Martínez, Paul, Lilian González-Chévez, and Andrés Fierro-Álvarez. 2004. "Endogenous Knowledge and Practice Regarding the Environment in a Nahua Community in Mexico." *Agriculture and Human Values* 21: 23–33.

Hilbert, Christopher. 2016. "'Anthropomorphismus!' als Totschlagargument: Anthropomorphismuskritik und Methodologie der Tierforschung." In *Den Fährten folgen: Methoden interdisziplinärer Tierforschung*, edited by Forschungsschwerpunkt 'Tier–Mensch–Gesellschaft', 277–292. Bielefeld: transcript.

Hildenbrand, Bruno. 2004. "Anselm Strauss." In *Qualitative Forschung: Ein Handbuch*, edited by Uwe Flick, Ernst von Kardorff, and Ines Steinke, 32–42. Reinbek: Rowohlt.

Hohmann, Katharina. 2012. *Lebensqualität im Altenheim: Zur Bedeutung tiergestüt-zter Dienstleistungen.* Bielefeld: MVV.

Honer, Anne. 2000. "Lebensweltanalyse in der Ethnography." In *Qualitative Forschung: Ein Handbuch*, edited by Uwe Flick, Ernst von Kardorff, and Ines Steinke, 194–203. Reinbek: Rowohlt.

Houde, Nicolas. 2007. "The Six Faces of Traditional Ecological Knowledge: Challenges and Opportunities for Canadian Co-Management Arrangements." *Ecology and Society* 12 (2): 34: 1–17.

Houwelingen-Snippe, Josca van, Thomas van Rompay, Menno De Jong, and Somaya Ben Allouch. 2020. "Does Digital Nature Enhance Social Aspirations?: An

Experimental Study." *International Journal of Environmental Research and Public Health* 17 (4): 1454.

Howard, Patrick, Catherine O'Brien, Brent Kay, and Kristin O'Rourke. 2019. "Leading Educational Change in the 21st Century: Creating Living Schools through Shared Vision and Transformative Governance." *Sustainability* 11 (4109): 1–13.

Hülst, Dirk. 2010. "Grounded Theory." In *Handbuch: Qualitative Forschungsmethoden in der Erziehungswissenschaft*, edited by Barbara Friebertshäuser, Antje Langer, and Annedore Prengel, 281–300. Weinheim: Beltz Juventa.

Hüther, Gerald. 2005. "Die Bedeutung emotionaler Bindungen an die Natur als Voraussetzung für die Übernahme von Verantwortung gegenüber der Natur." In *Naturerfahrung: Wege zu einer Hermeneutik der Natur*, edited by Michael Gebauer and Ulrich Gebhard, 219–233. Kusterdingen: SFG-Servicecenter Fachverlage GmbH.

Hüther, Gerald. 2008. "Das Erleben von Natur aus Sicht der modernen Hirnforschung." In *Kinder und Natur in der Stadt: Spielraum Natur: Ein Handbuch für Kommunalpolitik und Planung sowie Eltern und Agenda-21-Initiativen*, edited by Hans-Joachim Schemel and Torsten Wilke, 15–26. Bonn: Bundesamt für Naturschutz.

Humberstone, Barbara, Heather Prince, and Karla A. Henderson. 2016. *Routledge International Handbook of Outdoor Studies*. Abingdon, UK: Routledge.

Hunn, Eugene S. 2011. "Ethnozoology." In *Ethnobiology*, edited by Eugene N. Anderson, Deborah M. Pearsall, Eugene S. Hunn, and Nancy J. Turner, 83–96. New Jersey: Wiley-Blackwell.

Huth, Martin, Kerstin Weich, and Herwig Grimm. 2019. "Veterinarians between the Frontlines?!: The Concept of One Health and Three Frames of Health in Veterinary Medicine." *Food Ethics* 3: 91–108.

ICAR3R. 2019. *Culture of Care – Projekt*. https://www.uni-giessen.de/fbz/zentren/icar3r/projekte/cultureofcare

Interagency Advisory Panel on Research Ethic. 2018. Accessed May 25, 2020. https://ethics.gc.ca/eng/policy-politique_tcps2-eptc2_2018.html

Irvine, Leslie. 2004. *If You Tame Me: Understanding Our Connection with Animals*. Philadelphia: Temple University Press.

Jackson, Michael. 1998. *Minima Ethnographica: Intersubjectivity and the Anthropological Project*. Chicago: University of Chicago Press.

Jarass, Lorenz J. 2009. *Windenergie: Zuverlässige Integration in die Energieversorgung*. Berlin: Springer.

Jickling, Bob, Sean Blenskinsop, Nora Timmerman, Michael De Danann Sitka-Sage. 2018. *Wild Pedagogies: Touchstones for Re-Negotiating Education and the Environment in Anthropocene*. Cham: Palgrave Macmillan.

Johnson, Jane and Chris Degeling. 2012. "Animals-As-Patients: Improving the Practice of Animal Experimentation." *Between the Species* 15 (1): 43–58.

Jones, Edward E. and Richard E. Nisbett. 1972. "The Actor and the Observer: Divergent Perceptions of the Causes of Behaviour." In *Attribution: Perceiving the Causes of Behavior*, edited by Edward E. Jones, David E. Kanouse, Harold

H. Kelley, Richard E. Nisbett, Stuart Valins, and Bernard Weiner. Morristown: General Learning Press.

Jones, Owain. 2019. "Wer melkt die Kühe in Maesgwyn?: Animalische Landschaften und Affekte." In *NaturenKulturen: Denkräume und Werkzeuge für neue politische Ökologien*, edited by Friederike Gesing, Michi Knecht, Michael Flitner, and Katrin Amelang, 287–320. Bielefeld: transcript.

Jungert, Michael. 2010. "Was zwischen wem und warum eigentlich?: Grundsätzliche Fragen zur Interdisziplinarität." In *Interdisziplinarität. Theorie, Praxis, Probleme*, edited by Michael Jungert, Elsa Romfeld, Thomas Sukopp, and Uwe Voigt, 1–12. Darmstadt: WBG.

Jutras, Sylvie. 2003. "Go Outside and Play!" *Canadian Psychology* 44 (3): 257–266.

Kahlert, Joachim. 2005. "Umweltbildung." In *Handbuch politische Bildung*, edited by Wolfgang Sander, 430–441. Schwalbach: Wochenschau Verlag.

Kahn, Laura H., Bruce Kaplan, and James H. Steele. 2007. "Confronting Zoonoses Through Closer Collaboration between Medicine and Veterinary Medicine (As 'One Medicine')." *Veterinaria Italiana* Jan–Mar 43 (1): 5–19.

Kaldewey, David. 2008. "Eine systemtheoretische Rekonzeptualisierung der Unterscheidung von Natur und Gesellschaft." In *Die Natur der Gesellschaft: Verhandlungen des 33. Kongresses der Deutschen Gesellschaft für Soziologie in Kassel 2006*, edited by Karl-Siegbert Rehberg, 2826–2836. Frankfurt a. M.: Campus.

Kaldewey, David. 2011. "Das Realitätsproblem der Sozialwissenschaften: Anmerkungen zur Beobachtung des Außersozialen." *Soziale Systeme* 17 (2): 277–307.

Kappeler, Peter M. 2017. *Verhaltensbiologie*. Wiesbaden: Springer.

Kardorff, Ernst von. 1995. "Qualitative Forschung: Versuch einer Standortbestimmung." In *Handbuch qualitative Sozialforschung: Sozialforschung: Grundlagen, Konzepte, Methoden und Anwendungen*, edited by Uwe Flick, Ernst von Kardorff, Heiner Keupp, Lutz von Rosenstiel, and Stephan Wolff, 3–10. Weinheim: Beltz.

Kassam, Karim-Aly S. 2009. *Biocultural Indigenous Ways of Knowing: Human Ecology in the Arctic*. Calgary: University of Calgary Press.

Kelle, Udo and Susann Kluge. 1999. *Vom Einzelfall zum Typus*. Opladen: Leske + Budrich.

Kellert, Stephan R. and Edward O. Wilson. 1993. *The Biophilia Hypothesis*. Washington, DC: Island Press.

Kellert, Stephen R. 1997. *Kinship to Mastery: Biophilia in Human Evolution and Development*. Washington, DC: Island Press.

Kiepe, Juliane. 2004. *Ästhetische Inszenierung in der Ethnography: Bronislaw Malinowski im Spannungsfeld der Kulturen*. Frankfurt a. M./Berlin/Bern/Brussels/ New York/Oxford/Vienna: Peter Lang.

Kincheloe, Joe L. and Shirley R. Steinberg. 2008. "Indigenous Knowledge in Education: Complexity, Dangers, and Profound Benefits." In *Handbook of Critical and Indigenous Methodologies*, edited by Norman K. Denzin, Yvonna S. Lincoln, and Linda Tuhiwai Smith, 135–156. Los Angeles: SAGE Publications.

Kirksey, S. Eben and Stefan Helmreich. 2010. "The Emergence of Multispecies Ethnography." *Cultural Anthropology* 25 (4): 545–576.

Köchy, Kristian, Matthias Wunsch, and Martin Böhnert. 2016. *Maximen und Konsequenzen*. Freiburg/Munich: Verlag Karl Alber.

Kompatscher, Gabriela, Reingard Spannring, and Karin Schachinger. 2017. *Human-Animal Studies*. Münster/New York: UTB.

Kopnina, Helen. 2017. "Future Scenarios for Sustainability Education: The Future We Want?" In *Envisioning Futures for Environmental and Sustainability Education*, edited by Arjen E. J. Wals, Joseph P. Weakland, and Peter Blaze Corcoran, 19–29. Wageningen: Wageningen Academic Publishers.

Kosut, Mary and Lisa J. Moore. 2016. "Urban Api-Ethnographie: The Matter of Relations between Humans and Honeybees." In *Mattering: Feminism, Science and Materialism*, edited by Victoria Pitts-Taylor, 245–257. New York: New York Press.

Kubes, Tanja A. 2014. "Living Fieldwork: Feeling Hostess." In *Ethnographien der Sinne: Wahrnehmung und Methode in empirisch-kulturwissenschaftlichen Forschungen*, edited by Lydia M. Arantes and Elisa Rieger, 111–126. Bielefeld: transcript.

Kubes, Tanja. 2018. *Fieldwork on High Heels: Eine ethnographische Studie über Hostessen auf Automobilmessen*. Bielefeld: transcript.

Kuckartz, Udo. 2018. *Mixed Methods: Methodologie, Forschungsdesign und Analyseverfahren*. Wiesbaden: VS-Verlag für Sozialwissenschaften.

Kuhn, Thomas S. 1967. *Die Struktur wissenschaftlicher Revolutionen*. Frankfurt a. M.: Suhrkamp.

Kuhn, Melanie and Sascha Neumann. 2015. "Verstehen und Befremden: Objektivierungen des 'Anderen' in der ethnographischen Forschung." *Zeitschrift für qualitative Forschung* 1: 25–43.

Kurth, Markus, Katharina Dornenzweig, and Sven Wirth. 2016. "Handeln nichtmenschliche Tiere?" In *Das Handeln der Tiere: Tierliche Agency im Fokus der Human-Animal Studies*, edited by Sven Wirth, Anett Laue, Markus Kurth, Katharina Dornenzweig, Leonie Bossert, and Karsten Balgar. Bielefeld: transcript.

Krämer, Stephanie. 2019. "Von Menschen und Mäusen, die Wissen schaffen." Accessed August 6, 2019. https://www.laborjournal.de/rubric/essays/essays2019/e19_13.php

Kremer, Kerstin H. 2010. *Die Natur der Naturwissenschaften verstehen: Untersuchungen zur Struktur und Entwicklung von Kompetenzen in der Sekundarstufe I*. PhD diss., University of Kassel.

Kropp, Cordula. 2015. "'Enacting Milk': Die Akteur-Netz-Werke von 'Bio-Milch'." In *Verschwindet die Natur?: Die Akteur-Netzwerk-Theorie in der umweltsoziologischen Diskussion*, edited by Martin Voss and Birgit Peuker, 203–232. Bielefeld: transcript.

Kruger, Katherine A. and James A. Serpell. 2010. "Animal-Assisted Interventions in Mental Health: Definitions and Theoretical Foundations." In *Handbook on Animal-Assisted Therapy: Theoretical Foundations and Guidelines for Practice*, edited by Aubrey H. Fine, 579–588. London/Oxford/Boston/New York/San Diego: Academic Press.

Krumm, Volker. 1996. "Wann tut ihr endlich, was ich sage, und nicht, was ich mache?: Anmerkungen zum Versagen der Umweltbildung und was man dagegen tun kann." In *Situation, Handlung, Persönlichkeit: Kategorien wirtschaftspädagogischen Denkens: Festschrift für Lothar Reetz*, edited by Wolfgang Seyd and Lothar Reetz, 24–44. Hamburg: Feldhaus.

LaJoie, Kathleen R. 2003. *An Evaluation of the Effectiveness of Using Animals in Therapy*. Unpublished PhD diss., University of Louisville.

Lamnek, Siegfried. 2005. *Qualitative Sozialforschung: Lehrbuch*. Weinheim/Basel: Beltz Juventa.

Lange, Hellmuth. 2011. "Umweltsoziologie in Deutschland und Europa." In *Handbuch Umweltsoziologie*, edited by Matthias Groß, 19–53. Wiesbaden: Springer.

Latour, Bruno. 1995. *Wir sind nie modern gewesen: Versuch einer symmetrischen Anthropologie*. Frankfurt a. M.: De Gruyter.

Latour Bruno. 2008. *Reassembling the Social: An Introduction to Actor-Network-Theory*. Oxford: Oxford University Press.

Latour, Bruno. 2017. *Kampf um Gaia: Acht Vorträge über das neue Klimaregime*. Frankfurt a. M.: Suhrkamp.

Laux, Henning and Anna Henkel. 2018. *Die Erde, der Mensch und das Soziale: Zur Transformation gesellschaftlicher Naturverhältnisse im Anthropozän*. Bielefeld: transcript.

Law, John. 2004. *After Method: Mess in Social Science Research*. London: Routledge.

Leeming, Frank C., William O. Dwyer, Bryan E. Porter, and Melissa K. Cobern. 1993. "Outcome Research in Environmental Education: A Critical Review." *Journal of Environmental Education* 24 (4): 8–21.

Lehmann, Jürgen. 1999. *Befunde empirischer Forschung zu Umweltbildung und Umweltbewußtsein*. Opladen: Leske+Budrich.

Lennox, Robert J., Kim Aarestrup, Steven J. Cooke, Paul D. Cowley, Zhiqun D. Deng, Aaron T. Fisk, Robert G. Harcourt, Michelle Heupel, Scott G. Hinch, Kim N. Holland, Nigel E. Hussey, Sara J. Iversen, Steven T. Kessel, John F. Kocik, Martyn C. Lucas, Joanna Mills Flemming, Vivian M. Ngyen, Michael J. W. Stokesbury, Svein Vagle, David L. VanderZwaag, Frederick G. Whoriskey, and Nathan Young. 2017. "Envisioning the Future of Aquatic Animal Tracking: Technology, Science, and Application." *BioScience* 67 (10): 884–896.

Leontjev, Alexej N. 1973. *Probleme der Entwicklung des Psychischen*. Frankfurt a. M.: Athenäum-Fischer-Taschenbuch-Verlag.

Levinson, Edward M., Melanie Vogt, William F. Barker, Mary Renck Jalongo, and Pat Van Zandt. 2017. "Effects of Reading with Adult Tutor/Therapy Dog Teams on Elementary Students' Reading Achievement and Attitudes." *Society & Animals* 25 (1): 38–56.

Linkous Brown, Kimberly. 2006. "As It Was in the Past: A Return to the Use of Life-Capture Technology in the Aboriginal Riverine Fishery." In *Traditional Ecological*

Knowledge and Natural Resource Management, edited by Charles R. Menzies, 47–65. Lincoln/New York: University of Nebraska Press.

Lob, Reinhold E. 1997. *20 Jahre Umweltbildung in Deutschland: Eine Bilanz.* Cologne: Aulis.

Locke, Piers. 2012. *Elephant Training in Nepal: Multispecies Ethnography and Rites of Passage.* Christchurch: University of Canterbury.

Locke, Piers and Ursula Münster. 2015. *Multispecies Ethnography: Oxford: Oxford University Bibliographies.* https://www.researchgate.net/profile/Ursula _Muenster/publication/294872069_Multispecies_Ethnography/links/56c485f108a e736e7046ed77.pdf

Lofland, John, David Snow, Leon Anderson, Lyn H. Lofland. 2006. *Analyzing Social Settings: A Guide to Qualitative Observation and Analysis.* Belmont, CA: Wadsworth.

Lorimer, Jamie and Clemens Driessen. 2019. "Wilde Experimente in den Oostvaardersplassen: Zur Neubestimmung des Umweltschutzes im Anthropozän." In *NaturenKulturen: Denkräume und Werkzeuge für neue politische Ökologien,* edited by Friederike Gesing, Michi Knecht, Michael Flitner, and Katrin Amelang, 105–138. Bielefeld: transcript.

Lorz, Albert and Ernst Metzger. 2006. *Tierschutzgesetz: Tierschutzgesetz mit Allgemeiner Verwaltungsvorschrift, Rechtsverordnungen und Europäischen Übereinkommen sowie Erläuterungen des Art. 20a GG. Kommentar.* Munich: C.H. Beck.

Lude, Armin. 2006. "Natur erfahren und für die Umwelt handeln: Wirkung von Umweltbildung." *NNA-Berichte* 19 (2): 18–33.

Lude, Armin. 2001. *Naturerfahrung und Naturschutzbewusstsein: Eine empirische Studie.* Innsbruck/Vienna/Munich: Studien-Verlag.

Lüders, Christian. 2000. "Beobachten im Feld und Ethnography." In *Qualitative Forschung: Ein Handbuch,* edited by Uwe Flick, Ernst von Kardorff, and Ines Steinke, 384–401. Reinbek: Rowohlt.

Luhmann, Niklas. 1984. *Soziale Systeme: Grundriß einer allgemeinen Theorie.* Frankfurt a. M.: Suhrkamp.

Luhmann, Niklas. 1995. *Über Natur: Gesellschaftsstruktur und Semantik. Studien zur Wissenssoziologie der modernen Gesellschaft: Volume 4.* Frankfurt a. M.: Suhrkamp.

Luhmann, Niklas.1997. *Die Gesellschaft der Gesellschaft.* Frankfurt a. M.: Suhrkamp.

Luschi, Paolo and Paolo Casale. 2014. "Movement Patterns of Marine Turtles in the Mediterranean Sea: A Review." *Italian Journal of Zoology* 81 (4): 478–495.

Maack, Lisa. 2018. *Hürden einer Bildung für nachhaltige Entwicklung. Akteurinnen und Akteure zwischen Immanenz und Reflexivität.* Bad Heilbrunn: Verlag Julius Klinkhardt.

Maanen, John van. 1988. *Tales of the Field: On Writing Ethnography.* London: University of Chicago Press.

Mackert, Gabriele and Paul Petritsch. 2016. *Mensch macht Natur: Landschaft im Anthropozän: Humans Make Nature: Landscape of the Anthropocene.* Berlin: De Gruyter.

Madden, Raymond. 2014. "Animals and the Limits of Ethnography." *Anthrozoös* 27 (2): 279–293.

Madden, Raymond. 2017. *Being Ethnographic: A Guide to the Theory and Practice of Ethnography.* Melbourne: SAGE Publications.

Magallanes-Blanca, Claudia. 2015. "Talking About Our Mother: Indigenous Videos on Nature and the Environment." *Communication, Culture and Critique* 8 (2): 199–216.

Mahner, Martin and Mario Bunge. 2000. *Philosophische Grundlagen der Biologie.* Berlin: Springer.

Malone, Nicholas and Kathryn Oveden. 2017. "Natureculture." Accessed October 7, 2019. https://onlinelibrary.wiley.com/ doi/pdf/10.1002/9781119179313. wbprim0135

Manser, Marta B. 2016. "Wann ist ein Tier ein Tier?: Oder: Ist der Mensch besonders?" In *Tierisch!: Das Tier und die Wissenschaft: Ein Streifzug durch die Disziplinen,* edited by Meret Fehlmann, Margot Michel, and Rebecca Niederhauser, 23–32. Zürich: Vdf.

Markham, Annette and Simona Stavrova. 2016. "Internet/Digital Research." In *Qualitative Research,* edited by David Silverman, 299–243. London: SAGE Publications.

Marvin, Garry and Susan McHugh. 2014. "In It Together: An Introduction to Human-Animal Studies." In *Routledge Handbook of Human-Animal Studies,* edited by Garry Marvin and Susan McHugh, 1–9. London/New York: Taylor & Francis Ltd.

Mathews, Petra and Edeltraud Kaltenbach. 2011. "Ethnography: Auf den Spuren des täglichen Verhaltens." In *Qualitative Marktforschung in Theorie und Praxis: Grundlagen – Methoden – Anwendung,* edited by Gabriele Naderer and Eva Balzer, 148–162. Wiesebaden: Springer.

Mauss, Marcel. 2013. *Handbuch der Ethnographie.* Munich: Wilhelm Fink.

Mayntz, Renate. 2005. *Forschungsmethoden und Erkenntnispotential: Natur- und Sozialwissenschaften im Vergleich.* Cologne: Max-Planck-Institut für Gesellschaftsforschung. https://nbn-resolving.org/urn:nbn:de:0168-ssoar-418504

McConnell, Bernie, Rory Beaton, Ed Bryant, Colin Hunter, Phil Lovell, and Alisa Hall. 2004. "Phoning Home: A New GSM Mobile Phone Telemetry System to Collect Mark-Recapture Data." *Marine Mammal Science* 20: 274–283.

Mead, Margaret. 1966. "Neighborhoods and Human Needs." *Ekistics* 21(123): 124–126.

Mead, Georg H. 1980. "Über tierische Wahrnehmung." In *Gesammelte Aufsätze: Volume 1,* edited by Georg H. Mead and Hans Joas, 140–158. Frankfurt a. M.: Suhrkamp.

Michel-Fabian, Petra. 2010. "Naturschutz und Ethik: Eine Skizze." In *Herausforderung Biologie: Fragen an die Biologie - Fragen aus der Biologie,* edited by Johannes Fehrle, Rüdiger Heinz, and Kerstin Müller, 47–63. Berlin: LIT.

Middleton, Arthur D., Matthew J. Kauffman, Douglas E. McWhirter, John G. Cook, Rachel C. Cook, Abigail A. Nelson, Michael D. Jimenez, and Robert W. Klaver. 2013. "Animal Migration Amid Shifting Patterns of Phenology and Predation: Lessons from a Yellowstone Elk Herd." *Ecology* 94: 1245–1256.

Milbradt, Björn. 2003. "Der Mensch in der Natur: Paul Taylor." In *Ökologische Theorien: Fünfzehn Vorlesungen zur Einführung: Kritische Philosophie, Umweltsoziologie, Poetische Ausgänge*, edited by Andreas Nebelung, 68–83. Berlin: Focus-Verlag.

Milton, Kay. 2005. "Anthropomorphism or Egomorphism?: The Perception of Non-human Persons by Human Ones." In *Animals in Person: Cultural Perspectives on Human-Animal Intimacies*, edited by John Knight, 255–271. Oxford: Berg Publishers.

Milz, Helga. 2009. "Mensch-Tier-Beziehungen in der Soziologie." In *Gefährten–Konkurrenten–Verwandte: Die Mensch-Tier-Beziehung im wissenschaftlichen Diskurs*, edited by Carola Otterstedt and Michael Rosenberger, 236–256. Göttingen: Vandenhöck & Ruprecht.

Mitscherlich, Alexander. 1965. *Die Unwirtlichkeit unserer Städte*. Frankfurt a. M.: Suhrkamp.

Moodie, Susan. 2010. "Power, Rights, Respect and Data Ownership in Academic Research with Indigenous Peoples." *Environmental Research* 110: 818–820.

Moore, Lisa Jean and Mary Kosut. 2014. "Among the Colony: Ethnographic Fieldwork, Urban Bees and Intra-Species Mindfulness." *Ethnography* 15 (4): 516–539.

Morgan, Paul A. 2017. "Envisioning Education in the Anthropocene: Long-Range and Game-Changing." In *Envisioning Futures for Environmental and Sustainability Education*, edited by Arjen E. J. Wals, Joseph Weakland, and Peter Blaze Corcoran, 117–127. Wageningen: Wageningen Academic Publishers.

Müller, Anja. 2011. *'Ein gemeinsames Band umschlingt die ganze organische Natur':Georg Forsters und Alexander von Humboldts Reisebeschreibungen im Vergleich*. PhD diss., University of Berlin.

Muhametsafina, Alexandra, Jonathan D. Midwood, S. M. Bliss, Kevin M. Stamplecoskie, and Steven J. Cooke. 2014. "The Fate of Dead Fish Tagged with Biotelemetry Transmitters in an Urban Stream." *Aquatic Ecology* 48: 23–33.

Mütherich, Birgit. 2004. *Die Problematik der Mensch-Tier-Beziehung in der Soziologie: Weber, Marx und die Frankfurter Schule*. Münster: LIT.

Nagel, Thomas. 1974. "What Is It Like to Be a Bat." *Philosophical Review* 83 (4): 435–450.

Nebelung, Andreas. 2003. *Ökologische Theorien: Fünfzehn Vorlesungen zur Einführung: Kritische Philosophie, Umweltsoziologie, Poetische Ausgänge*. Berlin: Focus-Verlag.

Nicoll, Kate, Cindy Trifone, and William Ellery Samuels. 2008. "An In-class, Humane Education Program Can Improve Young Students' Attitudes toward Animals." *Society and Animals* 16 (1): 45–60.

Nitschke, August. 1999. "Das Tier in der Spätantike, im Frühen und Hohen Mittelalter." In *Tiere und Menschen: Geschichte und Aktualität eines prekären Verhältnisses*, edited by Paul Münch and Rainer Walz, 227–246. Paderborn: Schöning.

Noske, Barbara. 2008. "Speciesism, Anthropocentrism, and Non-Western Cultures." In *Social Creatures: A Human and Animal Studies Reader*, edited by Clifton P. Flynn, 77–87. New York: Lantern Books.

Nowosadtko, Jutta. 1999. "Zwischen Ausbeutung und Tabu: Nutztiere in der Frühen Neuzeit." In *Tiere und Menschen: Geschichte und Aktualität eines prekären Verhältnisses*, edited by Paul Münch and Rainer Walz, 245–274. Paderborn: Schöning.

O'Brien, Catherine. 2016. *Education for Sustainable Happiness and Well-Being*. New York: Routledge.

O'Brien, Catherine and Chris Adam. 2016. "Sustainable Happiness, Living Campus, and Wellbeing for All." *International Journal of Innovation, Creativity and Change* 2 (3): 57–70.

O'Brien, Catherine and Patrick Howard. 2016. "The Living School: The Emergence of a Transformative Sustainability Education Paradigm." *Journal for Education for Sustainable Development* 10 (1): 115–130.

O'Reilly, Karen. 2005. *Ethnographic Methods*. London: SAGE Publications.

O'Reilly, Karen. 2009. *Key Concepts in Ethnography*. London: SAGE Publications.

Ogden, Laura A., Billy Hall, and Kimiko Tanita. 2013. "Animals, Plants, People and Things: A Review of Multispecies Ethnography." *Environment and Society* (4): 5–24.

Okello, Anna L., E. Paul Gibbs, Alai Vandersmissen, and Susan C. Welburn. 2011. "One Health and the Neglected Zoonoses: Turning Rhetoric Into Reality." *Veterinary Record* 169 (11): 281–285.

Otterstädt, H. 1962."Untersuchungen über den Spielraum von Vorortkindern einer mittleren Stadt." *Psychologische Rundschau* 13: 275–287.

Otterstedt, Carola. 2003. "Kultur- und religionsphilosophische Gedanken zur Mensch-Tier-Beziehung." In *Menschen brauchen Tiere: Grundlagen und Praxis der tiergestützten Pädagogik und Therapie*, edited by Erhard Olbrich and Carola Otterstedt, 15–31. Stuttgart: Kosmos.

Otterstedt, Carola. 2009. "Die Mensch-Tier-Beziehung im interkulturellen Vergleich." In *Gefährten - Konkurrenten - Verwandte: Die Mensch-Tier-Beziehung im wissenschaftlichen Diskurs*, edited by Carola Otterstedt and Michael Rosenberger, 294–315. Göttingen: Vandenhöck & Ruprecht.

Panksepp, Jaak. 2005. "Affective Consciousness: Core Emotional Feelings in Animals and Humans." *Consciousness and Cognition* 14: 30–80.

Papadopoulos, Andrew and Sarah Wilmer. 2011. "One Health: A Primer." Accessed August 2, 2019. http://ncceh.ca/sites/default/files/ One_Health_Primer_Nov_2011 _0.pdf

Patronek, Gary J. 2008. "Hoarding of Animals: An Under-recognized Public Health Problem in a Difficult-to-Study Population." In *Social Creatures: A Human and Animal Studies Reader*, edited by Clifton P. Flynn, 207–219. New York: Lantern Books.

Paul, Elizabeth S. and Michael T. Mendl. 2018. "Animal Emotion: Descriptive and Prescriptive Definitions and Their Implications for a Comparative Perspective." *Applied Animal Behaviour Science* 205: 202–209.

Paxson, Heather. 2019. "Käsekulturen nach Pasteur." In *NaturenKulturen: Denkräume und Werkzeuge für neue politische Ökologien*, edited by Friederike Gesing, Michi Knecht, Michael Flitner, and Katrin Amelang, 259–287. Bielefeld: transcript.

Pedersen, Helena. 2010. *Animals in Schools: Processes and Strategies in Human-Animal*. Education, West Lafayette: Purdue University Press.

Pedersen, Helena. 2011a. "Animals and Education Research: Enclosures and Openings." In *Undisciplined Animals: Invitation to Animal Studies*, edited by Pär Segerdahl, 11–26. Newcastle: Cambridge Scholars Publishing.

Pedersen, Helena. 2011b. "Counting Affects: Mo(ve)ments of Intensity in Critical Avian Education." *Canadian Journal of Environmental Education* 16: 14–45.

Pedersen, Helena. 2011c. "Release the Moths: Critical Animal Studies and the Posthumanist Impulse." *Culture, Theory and Critique* 52: 65–81.

Perler, Dominik and Markus Wild. 2005. *Der Geist der Tiere: Philosophische Texte zu einer aktuellen Diskussion*. Frankfurt a. M.

Peuker, Birgit. 2011. "Akteur-Netzwerk-Theorie und politische Ökonomie." In *Handbuch Umweltsoziologie*, edited by Matthias Groß, 154–172. Wiesbaden: Springer.

Peternell, Marion. 2014. "Ein Bienenschwarm im Klassenzimmer." *Green Care* 2: 24–26.

Philipps, Mary T. 2008. "Savages, Drunks, and Lab Animals: The Researcher's Perception of Pain." In *Social Creatures: A Human and Animal Studies Reader*, edited by Clifton P. Flynn, 317–334. New York: Lantern Books.

Pierotti, Raymond. 2015. "Indigenous Concepts of 'Living Systems': Aristotelian 'Soul' meets Constructal Theory." *Ethnobiology Letters* 6 (1): 80–88.

Pierotti, Raymond and Daniel Wildcat. 2000. "Traditional Ecological Knowledge: The Third Alternative (Commentary)." *Ecological Applications* 10 (5): 1333–1340.

Pink, Sarah. 2015. *Doing Visual Ethnography*. 2nd ed. Los Angeles: SAGE Publications.

Plessner, Helmuth. 2003[1946]. "Mensch und Tier." In *VIII: Conditio Humana*, 4th ed., edited by Günther Dux, Odo Marquard, and Elisabeth Ströker, 52–65. Gesammelte Schriften 8. Frankfurt am Main: Suhrkamp.

Plessner, Helmuth. 2003[1950]. "Über das Welt- Umweltverhältnis des Menschen." In *VIII: Conditio Humana*, 4th ed., edited by Günter Dux, Odo Marquard, and Elisabeth Ströker, 77–87. Gesammelte Schriften 8. Frankfurt am Main: Suhrkamp.

Plessner, Helmuth. 2003[1953]. "Mit anderen Augen." In *VIII: Conditio Humana*, 4th ed., edited by Günther Dux, Odo Marquard, and Elisabeth Ströker, 88–104. Gesammelte Schriften 8. Frankfurt am Main: Suhrkamp.

Plumwood, Val. 2002. *Environmental Culture: The Ecological Crisis of Reason*. Abingdon: Routledge.

Pole, Christopher and Marlene Morrison. 2003. *Ethnography for Education*. Berkshire: Open University Press.

Preston, Christopher. 2019. *Sind wir noch zu retten?: Wie wir mit neuen Technologien die Natur verändern können*. Wiesbaden: Springer.

Preuß, Bianca. 2012. *(Hoch)Begabungsförderung für alle?: Die Leitidee der Hochbegabtenförderung als Inklusions-'impact' für individuelle Begabungsförderung und Schulentwicklung*. Wiesbaden: VS.

Pschera, Alexander. 2014. *Das Internet der Tiere*. Berlin: Mathes und Seitz.

Pyyhtinen, Olli. 2016. *More-than-Human Sociology: A New Sociological Imagination*. New York: Palgrave Macmillan.

Randler, Christoph. 2018. *Verhaltensbiologie*. Bern: UTB.

Ragin, Charles C. 1994. *Constructing Social Research*. Thousand Oaks/London/New Delhi: Pine Forge Press.

Raus, Rea and Thomas Falkenberg. 2015. "The Journey towards a Teacher's Ecological Self: A Case Study of a Student Teacher." *Journal of Teacher Education for Sustainability* 16 (2): 103–114.

Raus, Rea and Veli-Matti Värri. 2017. "Teacher Ecological Self: An Ontological Journey." In *Envisioning Futures for Environmental and Sustainability Education*, edited by Arien E. J. Wals, Joseph Weakland, and Peter Blaze Corcoran, 103–116. Wageningen: Wageningen Academic Publishers.

Rees, William E. 2003. "Impeding Sustainability?" *Planning for Higher Education* 31 (3): 88–98.

Regan, Tom. 1983. *The Case for Animal Rights*. Berkeley: University of California Press.

Reichhold, Josef H. 2016. *Evolution: Eine kurze Geschichte von Mensch und Natur*. Munich: Carl Hanser Verlag.

Rist, Stephan and Farid Dahdouh-Guebas. 2006. "Ethnosciences: A Step towards the Integration of Scientific and Indigenous Forms of Knowledge in the Management of Natural Resources for the Future." *Environmental Development and Sustainability* 8: 467–493.

Rock, Paul. 2001. "Symbolic Interactionism and Ethnography." In *Handbook of Ethnography*, edited by Paul Atkinson, Amanda Coffey, Sara Delamont, John Lofland, and Lyn Lofland, 26–38. Los Angeles: SAGE Publications.

Rosa, Hartmut. 2014. "Die Natur als Resonanzraum und als Quelle starker Wertungen." In *Welche Natur brauchen wir?: Analyse einer anthropologischen Grundproblematik des 21. Jahrhunderts*, edited by Gerald Hartung and Thomas Kirchhoff, 123–144. Freiburg: Karl Alber.

Roscher, Mieke. 2012. "Human-Animal Studies." *Docupedia-Zeitgeschichte*. Accessed August 8, 2020. http://docupedia.de/zg/roscher_human-animal_studies_v1_de_2012

Rousseau, Jean Jaques. 1978. *Emile oder über die Erziehung: Vollständige Ausgabe*. Paderborn: Ferdinand Schöningh.

Russell, William M. S. and Rex L. Burch. 1959. *The Principles of Humane Experimental Technique*. London: Methuen.

Russell, Lisa. 2005. "It's a Question of Trust: Balancing the Relationship between Students and Teachers in Ethnographic Fieldwork." *Qualitative Research* 5 (2): 181–199.

Russell, Lisa and Ruth Barley. 2020. "Ethnography, Ethics and Ownership of Data." *Ethnography* 21 (1): 5–25.

Samhita, Laasya and Hans J. Gross. 2013. "The 'Clever Hans Phenomenon' Revisited." *Communicative & Integrative Biology* 6 (6): e27122/1–e27122/3.

Sander, Kirsten. 2012. "Interaktionsordnungen: Zur Logik des Scheiterns und Gelingens professioneller Praxen." In *Interaktionsordnungen: Gesundheit und soziale Praxis*, edited by Andreas Hanses and Kirsten Sander, 15–34. Wiesbaden: VS Verlag für Sozialwissenschaften.

Sardello, Robert and Chery Sanders. 1999. "Care of the Senses: A Neglected Dimension of Education." In *Education, Information and Transformation*, edited by Jeffrey Kane, 223–247. New Jersey: Prentice Hall.

Sauvé, Lucie. 1996. "Environmental Education and Sustainable Development: A Further Appraisal." *Canadian Journal of Environmental Education* V1: 7–34.

Schatzmann, Leonard and Anselm L. Strauss. 1973. *Field Research: Strategies of Natural Sociology*. Englewood Cliffs, NJ: Prentice-Hall.

Schauder, Wilhelm. 1957. "Zur Geschichte der Veterinärmedizin an der Universität und Justus-Liebig-Hochschule." In *Gießen: Festschrift zur 350-Jahrfeier*, edited by Justus-Liebig-University Gießen, 96–173. Gießen: Schmitz.

Schimank, Uwe. 2010. *Handeln und Strukturen: Einführung in die akteurtheoretische Soziologie*. Weinheim/Munich: Juventa.

Schönhuth, Michael. 2018. "Ethnologie." In *Grundbegriffe der Soziologie*, edited by Johannes Kopp and Anja Steinbach, 95–97. Wiesbaden: Springer VS.

Schütz, Alfred. 1971. *Gesammelte Aufsätze I: Das Problem der sozialen Wirklichkeit*. Den Haag: Martinus Nijhoff.

Schulz, Marc. 2015. "'Sinnliche Ethnographie' als Fiktion und 'Augen-Ethnographie' als Praxis: Anmerkungen zum ethnografischen Wahrnehmen und Erkennen als epistemologisches Problem." *Zeitschrift für qualitative Forschung* 1: 43–55.

Schwabe, Calvin W. 1984. *Veterinary Medicine and Human Health*. Baltimore, MD: Williams & Wilkins Co.

Searles, Harold F. 1960. *The Nonhuman Environment in Normal Development and Schizophrenia*. New York: International Universities Press.

Sebastian, Marcel and Julia Gutjahr. 2013. "Das Mensch-Tier-Verhältnis in der Frankfurter Schule." In *Einleitung: Ambivalenzen in der Gesellschafts-Tier-Beziehung*, edited by Birgit Pfau-Effinger and Sonja Buschka, 97–119. Wiesbaden: Springer VS.

Sebastian, Marcel. 2017. "Deadly Efficiency: The Impact of Capitalist Production on the 'Meat' Industry, Slaughterhouse Workers and Nonhuman Animals." In *Animal Oppression and Capitalism: Vol. 2*, edited by David Nibert. Santa Barbara: Praeger Press.

Segerer, Andreas H. 2018. *Das große Insektensterben: Was es bedeutet und was wir jetzt tun müssen*. Munich: oekom.

Selby, David A. and Fumiyo Kagawa. 2015. "Drawing Threads Together: A Critical and Transformative Agenda for Sustainability Agenda." In *Sustainability Frontiers: Critical and Transformative Voices from the Borderlands of Sustainability Education*, edited by David Selby and Fumiyo Kagawa, 277–280. Leverkusen: Barbara Budrich Publishers.

140 *Works Cited*

Sempik, Joe, Rachel Hine, and Deborah Wilcox. 2010. *Green Care: A Conceptual Framework: A Report of the Working Group on the Health Benefits of Green Care.* Loughborough: Loughborough University. http://www.umb.no/statisk/greencare/green_carea_conceptual_framework.pdf

Serpell, James A. 1985. "Der beste Freund oder der schlimmste Feind: Haushund verändert sich je Kultur." *Institut für Interdisziplinäre Erforschung der Mensch-Tier-Beziehung*: 121–125.

Shah, Mira. 2020. *Affe und Affekt: Die Poetik und Politik der Emotionalität in der Primatologie.* Stuttgart: J.B. Metzler.

Shapiro, Kenneth J. 2008. "An Introduction to Human-Animal Studies." In *Social Creatures: A Human and Animal Studies Reader*, edited by Clifton P. Flynn, 3–6. New York: Lantern Books.

Shapiro, Kenneth J. and Margo DeMello. 2010. "The State of Human-Animal Studies." *Society and Animals* 18 (3): 307–318.

Simmel, Georg. 1993. "Soziologie der Sinne." In *Aufsätze und Abhandlungen 1901–1908: Band II. Band 8*, edited by Georg Simm, 276–292. Frankfurt a. M.: Suhrkamp.

Singer, Peter. 1975. *Animal Liberation.* New York: Avon.

Smartt Gullion, Jessica. 2016. *Writing Ethnography.* Rotterdam: Sense.

Smith-Harris, Tracey. 2003. "Bringing Animals into Feminist Critiques of Science." *Canadian Woman Studies* 23 (1): 85–89.

Snauwaert, Dale T. 2009. "Human Rights and Cosmopolitan Democratic Education." *Philosophical Studies in Education* 40: 94–103.

Sorge, Carmen. 2008. "The Relationship between Bonding with Nonhuman Animals and Students' Attitudes toward Science." *Society and Animals* 16 (2): 171–184.

Spannring, Reingard, Karin Schachinger, Gabriela Kompatscher, and Alejandro Boucabeille. 2015. "Einleitung." In *Disziplinierte Tiere?: Perspektiven der Human-Animal Studies für die wissenschaftlichen Disziplinen*, edited by Reingard Spannring, Karin Schachinger, Gabriela Kompatscher, and Alejandro Boucabeille, 13–28. Bielefeld: transcript.

Spittler, Gerd. 2001. "Teilnehmende Beobachtung als Dichte Teilnahme." *Zeitschrift für Ethnologie* 126: 1–25.

Spradley, James P. 1980. *Participant Observation.* New York: Holt, Rinehart & Winston.

Springer, Anna Sophie. 2016. "Der Anthropozän-Wortschatz." Accessed July 6, 2020. https://www.bpb.de/gesellschaft/ umwelt/anthropozaen/216925/das-woerterbuch-zum-anthropozaen

Stamp Dawkins, Marian. 2007. *Observing Animal Behavior: Design and Analysis of Quantitative Data.* Oxford: Oxford Press.

Statista. 2019. "Klimawandel: Statista-Dossier zum Thema Klimawandel 2018." Accessed August 24, 2020. https://de.statista.com/statistik/studie/id/41248/dokument/klimawandel-statista-dossier/

Stehr, Nico. 2019. *Gesellschaft und Klima: Entwicklungen, Umbrüche, Herausforderungen.* Weilerwist: Velbrück.

Steinbrecher, Aline. 2009. "In der Geschichte ist viel zu wenig von Tieren die Rede (Elias Canetti): Die Geschichtswissenschaft und ihre Auseinandersetzung mit den Tieren." In *Gefährten – Konkurrenten – Verwandte: Die Mensch-Tiererziehung als Menschenerziehung?: Tier-Beziehung im wissenschaftlichen Diskurs*, edited by Carola Otterstedt and Michael Rosenberger, 264–286. Göttingen: Vandenhoeck & Ruprecht.

Steinke, Ines. 1999. *Kriterien qualitativer Forschung: Ansätze zur Bewertung qualitativ-empirischer Sozialforschung*. Weinheim: Juventa.

Stewart, Laughlin, Evan L. MacLean, David Ivy, Vanessa Woods, Eliot Cohen, Kerri Rodriquez, Matthew McIntyre, Sayan Mukherjee, Josep Call, Juliane Kaminski, Ádám Miklósi, Richard W. Wrangham, and Brian Hare. 2015. "Citizen Science as a New Tool in Dog Cognition Research." *PLoS ONE* 10 (9). https://journals.plos.org/plosone/article?id=10.1371/journal.pone.0135176

Störk, Lothar. 1999. "Tiere im Alten Ägypten." In *Tiere und Menschen: Geschichte und Aktualität eines prekären Verhältnisses*, edited by Paul Münch and Rainer Walz, 87–119. Paderborn: Schöningh.

Straus, Erwin. 1963. *The Primary World of the Senses: A Vindication of Sensory Experience*. New York: Free Press of Glencoe.

Strauss, Anselm L. and Juliet Corbin. 1996. *Grounded Theory: Grundlagen Qualitativer Forschung*. Weinheim: Beltz.

Strauss, Anselm L. 1998. *Grundlagen qualitativer Sozialforschung*. Munich: Fink.

Strunz, Inge. 2013. "'Gibt es hier auch Tiere?': Oder: Der Beitrag der tiergestützten Pädagogik zum Lernen auf dem Bauernhof." In *Raus auf's Land: Landwirtschaftliche Betriebe als zeitgemäße Erfahrung- und Lernorte für Kinder und Jugendliche*, edited by Dorit Haubenhofer and Inge A. Strunz, 159–184. Baltmannsweiler: Schneider Verlag.

Sturm, H. 1974. "Beobachtung im Biologieunterricht: Ein Versuch zur Begriffsklärung." *MNU27* 6: 339–344.

Subcommission on Quaternary Stratigraphy. 2016. "Working Group on the 'Anthropocene' Current Definition." Accessed August 24, 2020. http://tinyurl.com/lhpzlrp

Subramaniam, Banu. 2019. "Meine Experimente mit der Wahrheit: Untersuchungen zur Biologie der Invasion." In *NaturenKulturen: Denkräume und Werkzeuge für neue politische Ökologien*, edited by Friederike Gesing, Michi Knecht, Michael Flitner, and Katrin Amelang, 175–202. Bielefeld: transcript.

Sukopp, Thomas. 2010. "Interdisziplinarität und Transdisziplinarität: Definitionen und Konzepte." In *Interdisziplinarität: Theorie, Praxis, Probleme*, edited by Michael Jungert, Elsa Romfeld, Thomas Sukopp, and Uwe Voigt, 13–30. Darmstadt: WBG.

Taylor, Affrica and Veronica Pacini-Ketchabaw. 2015. "Learning with Children, Ants, and Worms in the Anthropocene: Towards a Common World Pedagogy of Multispecies Vulnerability." *Pedagogy, Culture & Society* 23 (4): 507–529.

Taylor, Kathy, Nicky Gordon, Gill Langley, and Wendy Higgins. 2008. "Estimates for Worldwide Laboratory Animal Use in 2005." *Alternatives to Laboratory Animals* 36: 327–342.

Taylor, Andrea Faber, Frances E. Kuo, Frances E., and William C. Sullivan. 2001. "Coping with ADD: The Surprising Connection to Green Play Settings." *Environment and Behaviour* 33 (1): 54–77.

Tennie, Claudio. 2019. "Could Non-Human Great Apes Also Have Cultural Evolutionary Psychology?" *Behavioral and Brain Sciences* 42: E 184.

Teutsch, Gotthard. 1975. *Soziologie und Ethik der Lebewesen: Eine Materialsammlung.* Bern/Frankfurt a. M.: Lang.

Thomas, Stefan. 2019. *Ethnography: Eine Einführung.* Wiesbaden: Springer.

Tsing, Anna. 2019. "Jenseits ökonomischer und ökologischer Standardisierung." In *NaturenKulturen: Denkräume und Werkzeuge für neue politische Ökologien*, edited by Friederike Gesing, Michi Knecht, Michael Flitner, and Katrin Amelang, 53–82. Bielefeld: transcript.

Uexküll, Gudrun von. 1964. *Jakob von Uexküll: seine Welt und seine Umwelt.* Hamburg: Christian Wegner.

Underberg, Natalie M. and Elayne Zorn. 2013. *Digital Ethnography: Anthropology, Narrative, and New Media.* Austin: University of Texas Press.

Unger, Hella von. 2014. *Partizipative Forschung: Einführung in die Forschungspraxis.* Wiesbaden: VS-Verlag für Sozialwissenschaften.

Universität Gießen. 2018. "Zertifikatskurs tiergestützte Dienstleistungen." Accessed August 24, 2020. www.uni-giessen.de/tdw

Valley, Willi, Guopeng Fu, and Eduardo Jovel. 2017. "Preparing Students for Complexity and Uncertainty: Flexible Learning Strategies for Developing Environmental Professionals." In *Envisioning Futures for Environmental and Sustainability Education*, edited by Arien E. J. Wals, Joseph Weakland, and Peter Blaze Corcoran, 217–228. Wageningen: Wageningen Academic Publishers.

Vernooij, Monika A. and Silke Schneider. 2013. *Handbuch der tiergestützten Interventionen: Grundlagen, Konzepte, Praxisfelder.* Wiebelsheim: Quelle & Meyer.

Veterinarians without Borders/Vétérinaires sans Frontières – Canada. 2010. "One Health for One World: A Compendium of Case Studies." Guelph, ON: VWB – Canada. Accessed August 24, 2020. http://www.onehealthinitiative.com/ publi cations/OHOW_Compendium_Case_Studies.pdf

Wals, Arien E. J., Joseph Weakland, and Peter Blaze Corcoran. 2017. "Introduction." In *Envisioning Futures for Environmental and Sustainability Education*, edited by Arien E. J. Wals, Joseph Weakland, and Peter Blaze Corcoran, 129–140. Wageningen: Wageningen Academic Publishers.

Weber, Max. 1985. *Wirtschaft und Gesellschaft: Grundriss der verstehenden Soziologie.* Tübingen: Mohr.

Wellnitz, Nicole and Jürgen Mayer. 2008. "Evaluation von Kompetenzstruktur und -niveaus zum Beobachten, Vergleichen, Ordnen und Experimentieren." In *Erkenntnisweg Biologiedidaktik 7*, edited by Dirk Krüger, Annette Upmeier zu Belzen, Tanja Riemeier, and Kai Niebert, 129–144. Kassel: Universitätsdruckerei.

Whitehouse, Hilary, Felicia Watkin Lui, Juanita Sellwood, M.J. Barrett, and Philemon Chigeza. 2014. "Sea Country: Navigating Indigenous and Colonial Ontologies in Australian Environmental Education." *Environmental Education Research* 20 (1): 56–69.

Wiedenmann, Rainer E. 2009. *Tiere, Moral und Gesellschaft: Elemente und Ebenen humananimalischer Sozialität.* Wiesbaden: VS-Verlag für Sozialwissenschaften.

Wiek, Arnim, Lauren Withycombe, and Charles L. Redman. 2011. "Key Competencies in Sustainability: A Reference Frame-Work for Academic Program Development." *Sustainability Science* 6 (2): 203–218.

Wild, Markus. 2013. "Der Mensch und andere Tiere." In *Tiere: Der Mensch und seine Natur*, edited by Konrad P. Liessmann, 48–67. Vienna: Paul Zsolnay.

Willems, Herbert. 2000. "Erving Goffmans Forschungsstil." In *Qualitative Forschung: Ein Handbuch*, edited by Uwe Flick, Ernst von Kardorff, and Ines Steinke, 42–50. Reinbeck: rowohlt.

Wils, Jean-Pierre. 1999. "Das Tier in der Theologie." In *Tiere und Menschen: Geschichte und Aktualität eines prekären Verhältnisses*, edited by Paul Münch and Rainer Walz, 407–427. Paderborn: Schöningh.

Wilson, Edward O. 1984. *Biophilia: The Human Bond with Other Species.* Cambridge: Harvard University.

Wolcott, Harry F. 1990. "On Seeking – and Rejecting –Validity in Qualitative Research." In *Qualitative Inquiry in Education: The Continuing Debate*, edited by Elliot W. Eisner and Alan Peshkin, 121–173. New York: Teachers College Press.

WPCCC (World People's Conference on Climate Change). 2014. "Rights of Mother Earth." Accessed August 24, 2020. http://pwccc.wordpress.com/programa/

Wyre, Jen. 2009. "Beyond Pets: Exploring Relational Perspectives of Petness." *The Canadian Journal of Sociology* 34 (4): 1033–1064.

Yates-Doerr, Emely. 2019. "Kommt Fleisch von Tieren?" In *NaturenKulturen: Denkräume und Werkzeuge für neue politische Ökologien*, edited by Friederike Gesing, Michi Knecht, Michael Flitner, and Katrin Amelang, 203–232. Bielefeld: transcript.

Young, Tuma. 2018. "Ko'wey Net Biodiversity?" *Ecology & Action* 36 (1): 10–11.

Zarger, Rebecca K. 2011. "Learning Ethnobiology: Creating Knowledge and Skills about the Living World." In *Ethnobiology*, edited by Eugene N. Anderson, Deborah M. Pearsall, Eugene S. Hunn, and Nancy J. Turner, 371–387. New Jersey: Wiley-Blackwell.

Zinsstag, Jakob, Esther Schelling, D. Waltner-Toews, and Matthew Tanner. 2011. "From 'One Medicine' to 'One Health' and Systemic Approaches to Health and Well-Being." *Preventive Veterinary Medicine* 101 (3–4): 148–156.

Zivkovic, Sharon. 2017. "How Can Education for Sustainability Create a Systemic Change?" In *Envisioning Futures for Environmental and Sustainability Education*, edited by Arien E. J. Wals, Joseph Weakland, and Peter Blaze Corcoran, 169–180. Wageningen: Wageningen Academic Publishers.

Index

3Rs, 32

actor-network theory (ANT), 62–63. *See also* post-ANTalienation of nature, 2, 7
ambivalence: in the human-animal relationship, 34; tolerance, 6. *See also* constructions of animals
The American Veterinary Medical Association, 32
animal capital, 31
animal experiments, 32
animal-supported: education. *See* education, nature-and animal-based education; services, 24; therapy, 24
Anthropocene, 27. *See also* overcoming of anthropocentrism
anthropology: cultural anthropology, 52; social anthropology, 52
anthropomorphism, 68
art-based methods, 80

behavioral ecology. *See* ethology
biophilia hypothesis, 23
Burch, Rex L. *See* 3Rs

Chicago school, 52
Clever Hans effect, 30
constructions of animals, 17

constructivist, 14
Corbin, Juliet. *See* grounded theory
critical animal studies, 35
critical theory, 15
cultural diversity, 38
culture of care, 65

data storage, 90
demarcation, 2
dense descriptions, 58, 101–3
dichotomies, 6–7, 115
direct field access, 29
documentation, 97–102
Du-Evidenz (You-Evidence) by Geiger, 17

education: environmental education, 20, 21; inclusive education, 20; multispecies education, 25; nature- and animal-based education, 10; sustainable education, 20, 21, 65; transformative sustainable environmental education, 22
environmental awareness, 25
environmental sociology, 9, 15
equipment, 97
ethnographic analyses, 43
ethnographic data analysis, 58
ethnographic records, 52

About the Author

Katharina Ameli (PhD) is coordinator at the 3R Center as well as post-doctoral researcher and lecturer at the Chair of Socialization and Education at Justus-Liebig-University Giessen. Her research interests include human-animal studies with a focus on animal-assisted services and nature-based pedagogy as well as obstetric violence.